RENTON

Pictorial Research by Cynthia Barker

"Partners in Progress" by Nada Oakley

Produced in cooperation with the Greater Renton Chamber of Commerce

Windsor Publications, Inc.
Chatsworth, California

RENTON

WHERE THE WATER TOOK WING

AN ILLUSTRATED HISTORY

BY DAVID M. BUERGE

Windsor Publications, Inc.—History Books Division
Managing Editor: Karen Story
Design Director: Alexander D'Anca
Photo Director: Susan Wells
Executive Editor: Pamela Schroeder

Staff for *Renton: Where the Water Took Wing*
Manuscript Editors: Amy Adelstein, Jerry Mosher
Photo Editor: Robin Mastrogeorge
Senior Editor, Corporate Biographies: Judith L. Hunter
Production Editor, Corporate Biographies: Una FitzSimons
Customer Service Manager: Phyllis Feldman-Schroeder
Editorial Assistants: Kim Kievman, Michael Nugwynne, Michele Oakley, Kathy B. Peyser, Susan Schlanger, Theresa J. Solis
Publisher's Representative, Corporate Biographies: Forest Holman
Layout Artist, Corporate Biographies: C.L. Murray
Layout Artist, Editorial: Michael Burg
Designer: Thomas McTighe

Library of Congress Cataloging-in-Publication Data
Buerge, David M.
Renton, where the water took wing : an illustrated history / by David Buerge ; pictorial research by Cynthia Barker ; Partners in Progress by Nada Oakley. —1st ed.
p. cm.
Bibliography: p. 129
Includes index.
ISBN 0-89781-319-7
1. Renton (Wash.)—History. 2. Renton (Wash.)—Description—Views. 3. Renton (Wash.)—Industries. I. Barker, Cynthia. II. Oakley, Nada. III. Title.
F899.R46B84 1989
979.7'77—dc20 89-8983 CIP

Published 1989
Printed in the United States of America
First Edition

Windsor Publications, Inc.
Elliot Martin, Chairman of the Board
James L. Fish III, Chief Operating Officer
Michele Sylvestro, Vice-President/Sales-Marketing

FRONTISPIECE: Lake Washington is a great spot for a picnic dinner and a colorful sunset. Photo by Eric Draper

FACING PAGE: The Tonkins' store, pictured here around the turn of the century, sold groceries and other merchandise in Renton from 1884 to 1946, moving several times as the business grew. Ownership of the store stayed within the family for three generations. Today, the triangular Tonkin Park marks the location of the original store. Courtesy, Renton Historical Society and Museum

Contents

Acknowledgments

Writing a book is always a cooperative effort, and special credit and thanks are due many who helped with the research, who read the manuscript for its inevitable errors, and who gave me the benefit of their own experience and wisdom. Special thanks to Ernest Tonda, director of the Renton Historical Museum; Ethel Telban, curator; and Trudy Manley and Pearl Anderson, aides. To Stanley Greene, president of the Renton Historical Society; Bea Mathewson, vice president; Louise George, society secretary; Rose Gigli, membership secretary; and Rose Mary Greene, member. To Carla Rickerson, Susan Cunningham, Richard Engeman, and Gary Menges at the Suzzallo Library Special Collections, at the University of Washington. To Clark Petersen, library director of the Renton Public Libary. To K.F. Johnson, manager of the Renton Chamber of Commerce, and Jim Holman, history coordinator at the Chamber. To Margie Wickham, chairperson of the Renton Centennial Committee. To Cecile Maxwell, chairperson of the Duwamish Tribe. To the Reverend Wallace Wilson, pastor of the Highlands Community Church. To Robert McBeth, program chairman of the Renton Rotary. To Paul Spitzer, corporate historian of the Boeing Company. To Ron Olson of the Renton Engineering Department. To historian Daniel Peterson at Seattle Central Community College. To Dr. S. John Vukov, Flo Lentz, Charmaine Baker, Barbara Shinpoch, Chuck Pepka, and to many others too numerous to name who took the time to share their reminiscences, to all many thanks. But a very special thank-you is due my wife, Mary Anne, and my children, David John and Catherine Emily, for their encouragement and long-suffering patience during the many hectic months of this project.

Oxen were used to move loads of timber down the jolting, jarring skidroads. "Greasers" (center) were employed to ease the passage of these mighty logs, wielding long poles with greased ends to swab the skids. Courtesy, Renton Historical Society and Museum

Introduction

In the city of Renton, the main public library is built across the Cedar River. The Cedar is not a big river. Its headwaters lie less than 100 miles east in the Cascade Mountains, and it empties into Lake Washington little more than a mile below the library, but in the fall it is the scene of a remarkable and ancient drama. Then, big, crimson-backed salmon, many having migrated into the lake from the Pacific Ocean, muscle their way up the current, over rounded cobbles to spawn at the places of their birth. It is a drama that has been reenacted in the river for thousands of years, and the library is a wonderful place to observe its progress.

It is remarkable that this annual migration still occurs in a river that flows through the heart of a city of more than 35,000 people, through one of the most industrialized parts of the state. The Boeing Company builds jetliners here, and a host of manufacturing plants cluster nearby. Renton is located in the most densely populated part of the state. A few miles northwest of it are Seattle's 500,000 residents; northeast of it are Bellevue's 85,000. Renton is overshadowed by these imposing communities, but it retains its identity, just as the river in its midst husbands its salmon year after year.

Perhaps the most common view of Renton is that seen by commuters heading south along Highway 405 on their way to work. Boeing's huge assembly plant rises abruptly from the lake, a match for the hills that converge here.

Cities are often associated with buildings or features that seem to capture their essences. Seattle has its towering skyscrapers and its futuristic space needle. Bellevue has its shining glass towers, its mall. Many would choose the Boeing plant as Renton's hallmark, but first impressions are often deceiving. There is a more revealing feature near the center of town.

This is a broad stretch of park sporting athletic fields, playgrounds, swimming pools, a theater, the library, municipal buildings, and a museum. It is a busy part of town. Children play, take swimming lessons, and rehearse plays here. Citizens read in the library, conduct the city's business in city hall, visit the museum or, in the season, watch the salmon move up river. The fact that many of them work at the Boeing plant tells much about modern history and the region's economy, but the broad park and its civic amenities tell more about the city and the people who claim it as their home.

A long time ago the native people who lived on the river's upper reaches believed that if the salmon were harmed, they would transform themselves into birds and fly into the air. Since then the world those people knew has itself been transformed. The story of Renton told in this book is a story about that transformation and about the hopes and travails that accompanied it.

Economics dictate that small cities receive short histories, and, accordingly, this account is brief. Although the scale of events here may be smaller than those in a bigger place, the changes they mark are no less profound, and the impact they had on people's lives are as deep in any town as they are in a metropolis. Renton's history is a record of a community emerging from change, struggling with and mastering change, and being transformed by change. In Renton the very water took wing, and that is a story worth telling.

One key to a good wife's smooth-running household was a grocer who delivered, or who was at least accessible along the electric railway line. In such a competitive business, grocers like Thomas Harries offered not only a convenient location and delivery, but also the best sales prices, and other advertising inducements. Courtesy, Renton Historical Society and Museum

CHAPTER 1

Land of the Duwamish

The Wilkes expedition recorded the natural environment of the Puget Sound area in 1845. This illustration of Admiralty Inlet shows Mount Rainier in the background, and the pole in front is believed to have held Indian nets for catching ducks. Courtesy, Special Collections Division, University of Washington Libraries

It would be interesting to know what passed through Henry Tobin's mind the day he landed at the birthing place of Renton. It was early in 1853; he had traveled all the way up the river in a canoe, and we can be sure he was not alone. The native Duwamish inhabited villages all along the river, and it was common for their men to guide whites visiting their lands.

Tobin was from Maine, and if he stopped to sift through his fingers the rich bottom soil of this land, he may have recalled the rocky earth of home, and nodded. Yes, one could harvest more than field stones here; rock there was, but it was where it belonged, in the hills that rose above the river, crowned with timber so tall it took your breath away.

Tobin had found a wonderful place, one worth the trouble of leaving home and coming

West, and he staked his claim to a half-square-mile of it on behalf of himself and his wife, Diana, who would soon join him. Their claim was at the confluence of two streams: one, the Cedar River coming out of the Cascade Mountains; the other, a short stream draining a large lake to the north. (This lake, dubbed Geneva by an early explorer impressed with its hill-girt beauty, is known today, rather unromantically, as Lake Washington.) The river and the lake outlet each bore waters from extensive watersheds, and they met to form a deep, dark stream, the Black River.

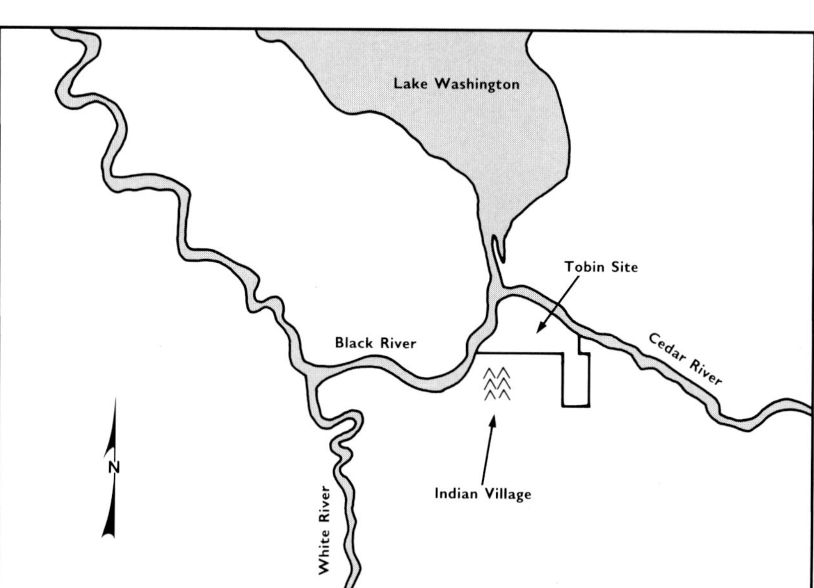

With the original courses of the Black and Cedar rivers shown here, the advantageous position of Henry Tobin's claim site can be seen. Directly south lay several Duwamish longhouses, which were excavated by archaeologists between 1979 and 1981. Courtesy, Renton Historical Society and Museum

Since disappeared, the Black River then flowed barely two miles before it joined another river, milky with sediment brought down from glaciers high up on Mount Rainier. Named the White River, it drained, like the two streams that formed the Black River, an extensive watershed. Together the Black and White rivers sired the Duwamish, which meandered down its narrow valley to Elliott Bay on Puget Sound.

Tobin had staked his claim strategically. The Black River was navigable; it served as an important link within a major river system. Furthermore the location commanded a confluence just below a lake.

To land speculators in nineteenth-century America, who had witnessed the success of confluence-towns like Pittsburgh and Cincinnati, such a spot was pure gold. In addition, the fact that the claim verged upon a lake conjured up images of Buffalo and Cleveland, each astride a river flowing into Lake Erie. To top it off, the Black River possessed a rapids (quickly advertised with more poetry than accuracy as Duwamish Falls), which, translated for speculators, meant a mill site.

Tobin must have smiled broadly as he hammered down the claiming stakes. No doubt about it: he had nailed a big one. It was a wonderful place, indeed.

It was also a richer one than he imagined. A few months later a new neighbor, Dr. R.H. Bigelow, working a claim south of Tobin's, discovered a coal seam. Bigelow was delighted; coal powered the wheels of industry and thus meant wealth for those who could supply it. Once he had calmed down he might have been astonished to learn that the material was at least 50 million years old. (In Bigelow's day many were still content with the belief that the earth itself was about 6,000 years old.) He would have been no less amazed to hear that the coal had been formed in a tropical climate, and probably would have branded as a lying fool anyone who ventured to tell him the land he was standing on had once been an island in the Pacific.

Such notions might not have seemed so far-fetched to the people whose lands Tobin and Bigelow had so heedlessly claimed, however. The Duwamish had lived beside the river for hundreds, perhaps thousands of years. They viewed the land differently than did the white settlers, and their myths about its creation bear a rough similarity to theories advanced by geologists today.

In one myth Muskrat creates the land by scooping up mud from beneath the waters and forming an island with it. In time this island grew, and the acts of other heroes gave it the character it has today. The original island, meanwhile, called *Sbah-bah-DEED* ("little mountain"), came to be identified as a hillock farther down the banks of the Duwamish River.

According to geologists, the rocky hills and coal seams of the Renton area were once lowlands on an island located somewhere in the tropical Pacific. Technically this island was a microcontinent, having a core of crystalline rock surrounded by an apron of sediment. This sediment nurtured lush tropical vegetation whose abundant remains, buried under material eroded from the high core, were transformed over time into layers of coal.

Transported atop a moving oceanic plate, as a box on a conveyor belt, this microcontinent moved northeast until, about 40 million years ago, it collided with the land mass of North America and became part of the continent. Today the crystalline core of this microcontinent forms the northern part of the Cascade Mountain range in Washington. The coal layers in the eastern part of the sedimentary apron are exposed near the towns of Roslyn and Cle Elum east of Snoqualmie Pass; those in the western part include the seam discovered by Bigelow.

The entire process took millions of years, during which the pressures generated by the collision and the continuing movement of the oceanic plate crumpled the edges of the microcontinent into a series of ridges. In the Renton area the axes of these ridges, which trend northwest to southeast, help determine the course of rivers flowing out of the Cascades, such as the Cedar River, which runs toward the northwest. East of Renton the highest of these ridges are known as the Issaquah Alps. In Renton, however, the ridges tend to be much lower and much more eroded, and parts of them are covered by younger glacial sediments. They reach the surface on the north bank of the Cedar River, on Renton and Talbot hills south of the Cedar, and on Earlington Hill, north of the old course of the Black River.

Another myth tells how, long ago, a powerful chief called North Wind dominated the land and covered it with ice and snow. Compare this with the theory of geologists positing that, beginning about 2 million years ago, great ice sheets formed in Canada expanded southward, covering the Puget Sound region. The ice, which reached nearly to where the town of Centralia is today, left behind thick deposits of sand, gravel, and clay when it retreated. This process, known as glaciation, occurred repeatedly. The most recent episode, which began about 18,000 years ago, gouged long deep troughs out of those earlier deposits. When the melting ice retreated about 12,000 years ago, sea water filled several of the exposed troughs, creating Hood Canal and Puget Sound.

One of the troughs was located east of Admiralty Inlet. Today it cradles Lake Washington and the Green River valley (the White River was diverted from the lower part of its channel in 1906, and its place was taken by the Green River), but 12,000 years ago it was an arm of the sea. (Remarkably, a Duwamish legend similarly recalls when Lake Washington was salt water.) Once the Cedar River delta, built with sediments carried out from the mountains, reached Earlington Hill, the Lake Washington basin was cut off from the sea, and streams entering the amputated arm created a freshwater lake. Sedimentation continued, meanwhile, as the Cedar River and overflow from the lake combined to form the Black River,

In 1980, an archeological dig was conducted at a longhouse site on the Earlington Golf Course. The dig provided key information about the Duwamish Indians, but later construction covered the site and made further excavation virtually impossible. Courtesy, Renton Historical Society and Museum

These remarkable pieces of ancient artwork, illustrated by Marilyn Morrison, represent animals familiar to the Duwamish, who originally carved them hundreds of years ago: an otter carved from bone (left); a siltstone bear (center); and a killer whale or sea lion chisled from nephrite (right). From Chatters, *Tualdad Altu: A Fourth Century Village on the Black River, King County, Washington*, 1988

which built its floodplain westward until it met that of the White. How long the process took is not clear, but it may have been accelerated by a catastrophe that occurred about 5,700 years ago.

At that time an eruption, similar perhaps to that which decapitated Mount Saint Helens in 1980, caused the summit of Mount Rainier to collapse, sending a tremendous avalanche roaring into the valleys of the White River and its west fork. Known as the Osceola Mudflow, the mass traveled at least 65 miles, burying more than 125 square miles of land under a blanket of rubble, and filling much of the White River valley.

A rocky knoll near the confluence of the Black and White rivers, known today as Surge Tank Hill, may have been one of the few places in the valley to survive, as an island of green amid the steaming gray waste. In fact, the Duwamish, who called the hill *Swah-wah-TEEH-tud* ("earth spirits"), believed it to be one of the few places that resisted the great transformation, the "turning-over" of the world, that ended the mythic age and ushered in the human era.

In time the scarred land healed. When the mudflow occurred the climate was stabilizing into the marine climate familiar today, mild and moist.

The moisture insured a luxurious growth of vegetation, cloaking the hills with tremendous stands of Douglas fir, western red cedar, and western hemlock, intermixed with red alder and big-leaf maple. In clearings appeared prairies rife with grasses and hardhack, and beneath those parts of the forest canopy through which sunlight was able to penetrate could be found a thick understory of shrubbery, much of it producing nuts and berries. In gloomier interiors the floor was dotted with ferns and mosses. On the floodplains below, where the ground was often saturated, black cottonwood and willow rooted in natural levees along with maple, alder, Oregon ash, Pacific crabapple, and wild cherry. Salmonberry, wild rose, thimbleberry, wild gooseberry, and red elderberry grew in rank profusion beside meadows spring-dappled with wildflowers. Swamps and marshes were thickset with broad cattail fields backed by tangles of hardhack and willow. Other water margins were carpeted with water lilies and leafy clumps of wapato with its succulent root.

Such dense greenery supported abundant wildlife. Elk grazed and deer browsed in clearings, and bears gathered berries in woodlands where mountain beavers dug their long burrows. Squirrels and chipmunks scolded in trees among whose shadows weasels darted furtively. In the wetlands where beaver and muskrat built their lodges, raccoons, otters, and skunks hunted. In turn, many of these creatures were preyed upon by wolves, mountain lions, and lynx.

Even the air was alive with life, especially in the spring and fall when millions of waterfowl migrated into the area, filling the air with their cries. The bird population ranged in size from tiny jeweled hummingbirds to giant condors who shadowed the land with 10-foot wingspans.

But the greatest and most significant animal populations were fish. These included resident stocks of suckers, trout, and peamouth. At certain times of the year the rivers were crowded with at least eight species of anadromous migratory fish that had been born in freshwater, migrated out to sea, and returned at maturity to spawn in the waters of their birth. These included trout and smelt, but most important were the salmon: the king, coho, and chum that spawned in the river gravels and the sockeye that collected in Lake Washington for two months before going up the river to spawn. Lake Washington also periodically swelled with migratory stocks: suckers, landlocked smelt, and a landlocked sockeye known as the kokanee that native fishermen considered a delicacy.

It was a wonderful place, and for the Duwamish it had been home for as long as they could remember. They had even taken their name from the river. To them, the Duwamish, Black, and Cedar rivers were all one stream, the Duw ("inside"), which is where the river took those who traveled it. Those who lived beside it and who drew their living from it were called *Duw-AHBSH* ("inside people"), a name since anglicized into *Duwamish.* Though a general term, it was applied specifically to the inhabitants of an important village on the Black River, who were said to be the "real" Duwamish. They dominated the most important link in the river system, a position which assured them great influence. Tobin and his friends were not the first to appreciate the lessons of geography.

These lessons had in fact been appreciated at least 1,600 years ago. Archaeologists in 1981 excavated the partially preserved floor of a fourth-century longhouse that had stood on the riverbank. The house appears to have been somewhat over 50 feet long and possibly 30 feet wide. Among the artifacts recovered there were a number of projectile points which had been chipped off petrified wood from the Columbia Plateau east of the mountains, and what seems to be a killer whale effigy carved from nephrite, a variety of jade, presumably from British Columbia. Other carved pieces included a bone animal figure and a small, freestanding quadruped, possibly a wildcat.

Because such accomplished artistry is typically the product of leisure time, the house would appear to have sheltered a relatively affluent group. The fact that the materials from which the objects were formed originated from east of the mountains and from British Columbia suggests the group enjoyed distant connections. It is likely they were the ancestors of the historic Duwamish who lived astride a trade route reaching from the continental interior to Alaska.

The Duw received waters from several streams, and the people living alongside them were the "real" Duwamish's nearer relations. In historic times the name *Duwamish* was applied

This detailed 1841 drawing of a Chinook lodge interior, which was similar to the longhouses of the Duwamish, shows a cooking fire and strips of salmon drying in the rafters above. Courtesy, Special Collections Division, University of Washington Libraries

Archaeologists have re-created the appearance of Duwamish longhouses, depicted in this detailed illustration by James C. Chatters. The longhouses consisted of cedar planking and flat roofs, supported by interior posts. From Chatters, *Tualdad Altu: A Fourth Century Village on the Black River, King County, Washington*, 1988

to them generally, though each had their own local name as well. All together they constituted but one of many groups living in the Puget Sound region that ethnographers have labeled Puget Salish. To the south were the Puyallup, to the west the Suquamish, and to the north and northeast the Snohomish and Snoqualmie. With the exception of the Suquamish, who inhabited islands and the western shore of central Puget Sound, the rest lived along rivers that today retain the names of these peoples.

The Duwamish's eastern neighbors were the Wenatchee and the Yakima who lived across the mountains, plateau people whose lives were different in many ways from those of the Puget Salish.

The village of the "real" Duwamish was made up of longhouses standing on both banks of the Black River, near the site of what is now the Renton Shopping Mall. A longhouse was a large frame structure sheathed with hand-hewn cedar planks that sheltered several related families. These families made up a house group, a self-sufficient economic unit who shared food and spent the winter months under a single roof. One cluster of longhouses was located on the north bank at a place called *Sbah-bah-DEED* ("little mountain") where the river had excavated cliffs from the toe of Earlington Hill. Across on the south bank a small stream called *Tu-hu-DEE-du* ("little Duw") entered just above the rapids, and several longhouses clustered near its mouth. Today this stream is called Talbot Creek.

Together the longhouses at *Sbah-bah-DEED* and at the mouth of *Tu-hu-DEE-du* made up a winter village group: a collection of dwellings whose members were united by kinship and residence and were exogamous; that is, who married partners from other winter village groups. This practice broadened the group's economic base, as the rights to gather food at certain areas were passed down family lines and distributed through marital ties. A member of one village group who married into another retained the identity of the original group, and when dead was buried in that group's burial ground. The burial ground of the aforementioned winter village was on the slope of Earlington Hill above *Sbah-bah-DEED*.

Below this winter village, at the confluence of the Black and White rivers, stood another whose main house site was located at a place called *Sko-AHK-ko* ("confluence"). Above, at the confluence of the Cedar River and the Lake Washington outlet, was found the winter village of a group called the *Skah-TELB-shahbsh* ("Skah-TELB people"). Talbot Creek was said to divide this group from the Duwamish at *Tu-hu-DEE-du*.

RIGHT: The bounty of the Puget Sound is displayed at this family's summer camp in the early 1900s. The dried fish and clams would later be stored for winter food. Courtesy, Special Collections Division, University of Washington Libraries

The *Skah-TELB-shahbsh* had longhouses at as many as four locations, although they may not all have been occupied at the same time. The first, at *Skah-TELBSH*, just west of where Renton High School is located today, derived its name from the *Skai-TAW*, a supernatural being described as having the size and shape of a man with very long hair, who lived in a deep hole in the river. A person who wished to become wealthy would ceremoniously wash himself, fast for five days, and dive to the bottom of the pool to meet with the *Skai-TAW*. As an embodiment of wealth, the *Skai-TAW* was also symbolic of the river's capacity to sustain life, since during their migrations, salmon congregated in its deep pools.

Another house site was located a short distance farther up the river at a place called *Tu-kwah-KWAH-chahb* ("little dogfish"). This was the haunt of another supernatural being whose movements were believed to cause the earth nearby to shake. *Tu-kwah-KWAH-chahb* may have been near a quaking bog, perhaps part of an abandoned slough.

Upriver from this spot, right at the confluence, was located the house site of *Twhahb-KO* ("murky water"), while up the Cedar River another house site was found at *Spah-DEL-gwelh* ("lots of dust on the riverside"). Both names may have described a single phenomenon: a silty section of river bank that had caved in as it was undercut, giving the water here and below a cloudy cast that also inspired the name for the Black River.

Another house site belonging possibly to the *Skah-TELB-shahbsh* was located on the lakeshore at a place called *Suh-TEE-cheeb* ("place where one wades") in what is now Bryn Mawr. A longhouse belonging to another winter village group stood on the lakefront at modern-day Kennydale, at a place called *Pah-sah-weh-eh* ("bent like a stick or tree"). Its inhabitants were *Shu-bahl-tu-AHBSH* who drew their names from *Shah-BAHL-tu* ("place where things are dried"), a house site at the mouth of May Creek. In all there may have been as many as 27 winter villages throughout the entire Duwamish River drainage. Those located within what are now the Renton city limits may have had a population that numbered 300-400, though of all the winter villages the one on the Black River, the village of the "real" Duwamish, was the most significant.

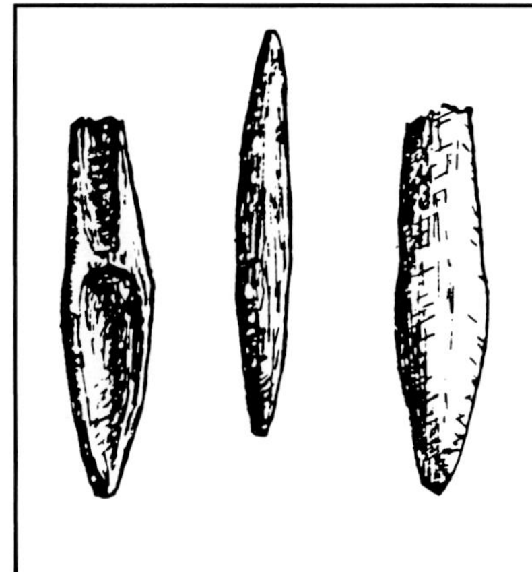

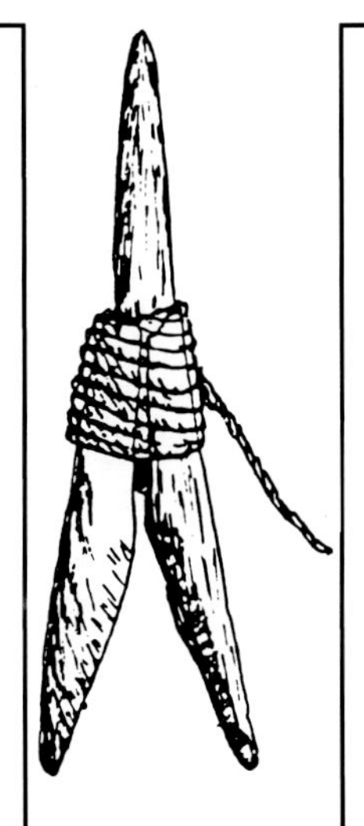

A variety of harpoons and their barbed points used by Duwamish fishermen were discovered at Tualdad Altu, a fourth century village site along the Black River. From Chatters, *Tualdad Altu: A Fourth Century Village on the Black River, King County, Washington*, 1988

The life these people lived took its rhythms from those of nature. The Duwamish year began when the first green shoots appeared in the woods outside the longhouses, dank and smoky after a winter's habitation. Salmonberry shoots and fern fiddleheads provided a welcome variation to a diet of last season's dried salmon and root mash. Gradually the house groups broke up, as family members ventured out of doors to their designated tasks: the men to hunt elk grazing in the swamps on bright yellow skunk cabbage, the women to dig camas bulbs in the greening meadows.

In April many families headed down the river to troll for salmon in the bay and to dig clams. By June, once the spring floods had subsided, men began building great tripod weirs on river bends where fishing was best. The Duwamish were able to entrap all the fish coming up the river if they so chose, but they understood the dangers of such action. Instead, the fishery was skillfully managed. Limits to the time weir screens remained in the water were agreed on to insure that the needs of upstream groups would also be provided for. In addition, the space between screen staves was adjusted to permit the fish below a certain size to pass through.

The idea of catching more fish than were

An impressive display of native American spirit boards, once used in tribal rituals, was collected for the Alaska-Yukon-Pacific Exposition in 1901. Courtesy, Special Collections Division, University of Washington Libraries

necessary, much less all of them, was repugnant to the Duwamish because they believed the creatures had a supernatural origin. Their coming was seen as the fulfillment of a promise the Salmon People had made in mythic times to the Changer, the demiurge whose heroism had made the world habitable. The Salmon People had promised the Changer they would surrender their robes of flesh to humankind if the latter would honor them for their sacrifice. This was done ritually, by performing ceremonies once the first fish of the season were caught and by taking only as many fish as were necessary. If the fish were dishonored they might refuse to return—and the people would starve.

The fish traveled a long road from the sea all the way up the Cedar River to the barrier of Cedar Falls. Fish were found also above the falls in Cedar Lake, apparently a relict population left over from the Ice Age, when drainage patterns were different. The fish in this lake were especially jealous of their mythic prerogatives. It was said that if they were abused they would sprout wings, turn into swans, and fly away. A provocative legend, it underscored the fact that abundance could not be taken for granted. The environment was the basis of survival; if it were not respected, its provisions would certainly disappear.

In the late summer and fall, when the salmon were running thickly, they were caught at night by the light of pitch fires or the full moon. A weir extended across the river, like a fence supported by log tripods. Unable to swim

This salmon weir observed by the Wilkes expedition along the Chehalis River in 1845 is similar to the ones built by the Duwamish on the Black and Cedar rivers. Courtesy, Special Collections Division, University of Washington Libraries

past this obstruction, the fish milled about on one side, while men stationed on platforms scooped them out of the water with dipnets and dropped them into canoes stationed on the other side. Taken ashore, the catch was gutted, cleaned, and hung on racks to dry in the sun or over slow-burning bark fires.

High summer was also a time for get-togethers. Yakimas rode over the mountains on their cayuse ponies to fish and trade with their western kin, and from out on the ocean coast, high-prowed canoes nosed their way upriver to exchange shells, oil, and slaves for fish, clams, loaves of dried berries, and mountain goat wool. Potlatches might be held to solemnize a marriage or to announce the assumption of a noble ancestral name. There would be gambling, athletic events, and perhaps a horse race on courses predating today's Longacres race track.

In November when the runs ceased and the rains came, the families reassembled in their longhouses. This was *SPEEG-pee-gwud* time, the time for "power singing," when the people's guardian spirits returned to them. The spirits had been traveling about the periphery of the world, and now they rejoined their hosts. Most spirits had been obtained as guardians during pubertal vision quests. Some of the spirits might be responsible for character traits such as bravery and humor; others provided skills or caused individuals to acquire wealth, and still others manifested themselves in ceremonial behavior. These latter ones prompted the people who had obtained them to announce a "power sing," an event when a person would ceremoniously sing the song the spirit had taught. Kin were invited to join in the singing and to wit ness awesome events: handling fire, inflicting wounds on one's self that healed miraculously, and causing inanimate objects to come to life. These were deeply religious events, but also occasions for visiting, feasting, and gift-giving.

The winter solstice heralded the coldest time of the year when the very young, the old, and the ill were most likely to die. It was thus believed to be a dangerous time, when the trail to the land of the dead opened wide and when ghosts moved among the living, eager to kidnap souls.

Symptomatic of soul-theft was loss of property, and if someone were so diagnosed, a remarkable "spirit canoe" ceremony that could last as long as five nights was performed. During this ceremony shamans dramatized a journey to the land of the dead from which they retrieved the soul, followed by a return trip in which they accompanied the soul back to its owner.

By reciting myths and dramatizing the actions of mythic figures, the cold was hurried away, and life was restored to the sleeping earth. Around February the frogs began to sing, and once again green fledged the sterile husk of the world.

It had happened this way since mythic times, since before memory in this wonderful place, since the Changer won the world for the Duwamish. But now a new season would bring word of new things, of a new people, and prophecies of a world about to change.

Most native American tribes had a unique method and design in creating their own distinct basketry. The designs on baskets woven by the Duwamish women represented patterns from nature or special patterns given by spirits, and the method most used by the Duwamish was the coiled weave technique. Courtesy, Special Collections Division, University of Washington Libraries

CHAPTER 2

Reaping the Riches of the Land

Mining, lumber, and agriculture were major business concerns in the early years of Renton's development. In agriculture, hops was an important cash crop in the surrounding valleys. By 1892, however, a hop blight had decimated most of the fields and harvests became spotty. The harvest at the Earlington hop field may very well have been the last in the area. Courtesy, Renton Historical Society and Museum

On May 19, 1792, British Captain George Vancouver anchored the H.M.S. *Discovery* off Bainbridge Island, a few months shy of the tricentennial of Columbus' discovery of the New World. Like his predecessor, Vancouver was also on a voyage of discovery, and his observations of the inlet he named after one of his lieutenants, Peter Puget, are the first on record.

During the next few days the explorers were visited by native traders who rowed out to the ship in high-prowed canoes. On May 22 nearly 80 others approached the *Discovery*; their canoes, unlike those previously, were shy of high bow and stern pieces. These natives made a favorable impression on the fastidious Vancouver, who judged them "infinitely more cleanly" than the earlier traders.

These latter visitors were probably the

Duwamish, who, as we know from later observers, traveled down the river in April in shovel-nosed canoes to troll for salmon on the bay. They traded bows and arrows and some garments for copper sheets, bells, and brass buttons from the ship's stores.

Western trade goods became more common after 1800, when traders began to frequent the region, and in 1832 full-scale trade on Puget Sound was initiated with the building of Fort Nisqually by the Hudson's Bay Company. The fort's *Journal of Occurrences,* kept by company clerks, often makes mention of the Duwamish trading furs for kettles, hatchets, clothing, guns, and a host of other goods.

In 1979 archaeologists found the remains of some of these goods at *Sbah-bah-DEED.* The items were scattered about the floor of a longhouse judged to have been about 25 feet wide and 80 feet long. The dwelling's interior hearth arrangement indicates a shelter for five families. Blue glass beads, copper, and other artifacts suggest that the house was occupied between 1790 and 1825.

Among the more interesting finds at the longhouse were copper fishhooks that were probably manufactured by a local coppersmith. This craftsman cut strips from a copper sheet by incising a groove on its surface and bending the sheet back and forth until the strip snapped off. Folded and twisted, the heated strip was hammered into a wire that was then bent into the shape of a hook. Other hooks were fashioned from iron nails.

Archaeologists plotted the position of each artifact in an effort to create a detailed picture of ancient life in the Duwamish longhouses. This site map, illustrated by James C. Chatters, shows the different living areas uncovered at the 45K159 Earlington dig. From Chatters, *Tualdad Altu: A Fourth Century Village on the Black River, King County, Washington,* 1988

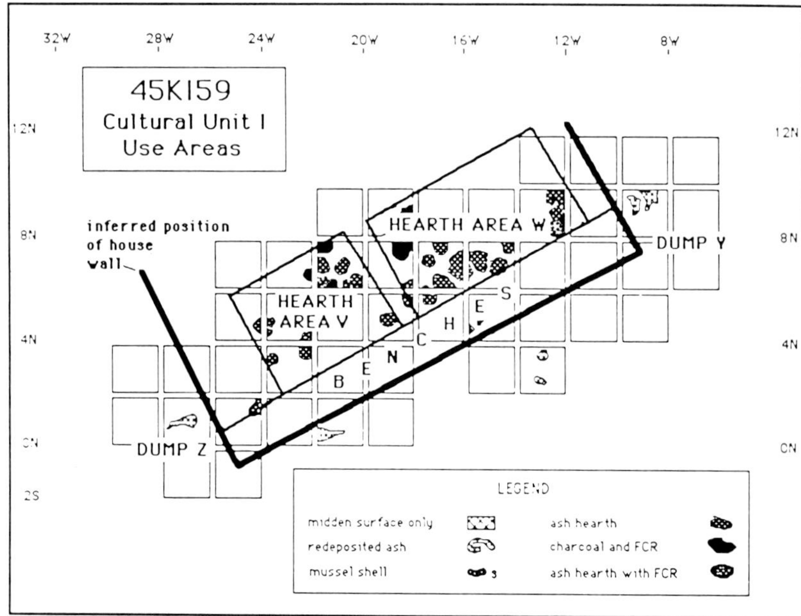

Most of the copper, iron, stone, and bone implements were found along the house margin, while beads were more common in the center. From this distributive pattern, it can be speculated that men sat on benches along the sides of the house as they made their tools, while women wearing beads gathered at the center, where cooking fires were located. We can imagine the children nestling in their mothers' laps, playing with the colorful bead necklaces until the strings broke and the beads showered onto the floor and were buried in the dust.

Tools and beads were not the only new items brought into the region by the Europeans. Horses had already revolutionized life in the interior, and guns were bringing increased violence to the coast. More devastating, however, were diseases such as typhoid and smallpox that ravaged native populations, particularly in seaside villages. It is not known if the Duwamish were directly affected by the epidemics, but they were caught up in the movements that appear to have followed them.

Some time between 1810 and 1825, the longhouse at *Sbah-bah-DEED* was abandoned in a fairly orderly manner. About this same period, according to Duwamish folklore, five families from the Black River migrated to a site on the lower White River where a huge logjam blocked river travel and created a natural fish-weir. The wealth and technical skill of the *Sbah-bah-DEED* longhouse-dwellers qualified them as local nobility, and they appear to have been the migrating group, perhaps filling a vacuum created by the disappearance of earlier inhabitants.

Not all the Duwamish left the main village site, however. Among those who stayed was *Kwi-AHK-teed,* a wealthy man said to have owned 20 slaves, purchased with lengths of dentalium shell traded in from the north, and two wives. He became a headman, sired many sons, and maintained ties with the lower White River group, the Suquamish, and the Snoqualmie. When he died an old man in the 1850s, several of his sons provided the Duwamish with leadership.

Among the *Skah-TELB-shahbsh,* the headman *Elk-klah-kum* wielded great influence. He appears to have been a Yakima who, like other members of this powerful group, succeeded in marrying into an important river family. Other notable families lived in the area, some of whom had taken Christian names such as Moses and Solomon. These names suggest the efforts of Catholic priests who carried out missions in the area beginning in 1840. The message they preached had an impact on the lives of their audiences as great as the goods introduced by traders.

A Methodist mission party led by American John Richmond reached Fort Nisqually in 1840, but the mission closed in 1842. In 1845, however, George Washington Bush, a black, led the 31-member Bush-Simmons group to the head of the Sound. Four years later, 19-year old John Holgate staked the first claim in the Duwamish River valley. In that same year, 1849, an energetic immigrant from Missouri, Isaac Neff Ebey, explored the eastern shore of the Sound and described it in an 1850 letter to Simmons. Published in the *Oregon Spectator* on October 17, 1850, it is the first printed account of the future site of Renton. Describing the land around the "Dewams" river, he wrote:

The river meanders along through rich bottom land, not heavily timbered, with here and there a beautiful plain of unrivalled fertility, peeping out through a fringe of vine maple, alder and ash, or baldly presenting a full view of their native richness and undying verdure. Other plains of more extensive character are represented as being near at hand, and of sufficient fertility to satisfy the most fastidious taste. At a distance of about twenty miles from the bay, the river forks—the right fork bears the name Dewams. It has its source about ten miles to the north in a large clear lake. This stream has an average width of about twenty yards. The country along its banks partakes of the same character as that lower down the river. A few miles of this stream will be found quite rapid, offering very fine opportunities for mill privileges. Sandstone of good quality for building material makes it appearance along the stream.

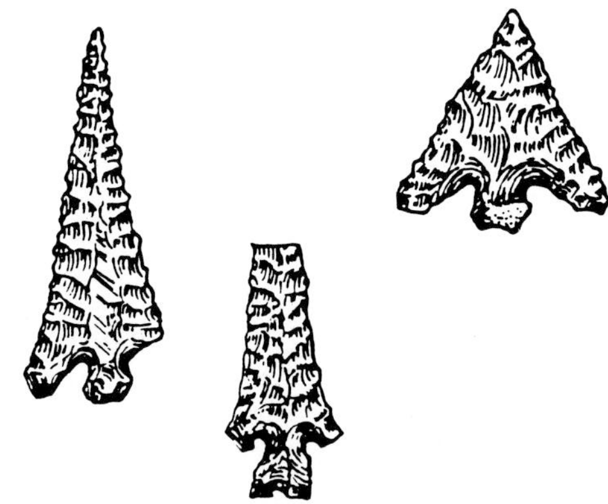

A selection of arrowheads, depicted in these illustrations by Marilyn Morrison, was excavated from a Duwamish longhouse site. They included these basal-notched, expanding stemmed, projectiles. From Chatters, *Tualdad Altu: A Fourth Century Village on the Black River, King County, Washington*, 1988

It was Ebey who christened the lake, Lake Geneva.

Ebey's account attracted attention. Soon several homesteads appeared in the Duwamish River valley, and on November 13, 1851, the Denny party from Illinois landed at Alki Point west of Elliott Bay. Unlike earlier pioneers, these new immigrants were interested in building a town, and soon there were two settlements: New York Alki on Alki Point, and Seattle on the bay's east shore, each eagerly soliciting the trade of those entering or departing the river.

Of all these pioneers, none appears to have impressed old *Kwi-AHK-teed* more than Arthur Denny, at 27 the patriarch and leader of the group that founded Seattle. At some point during the uncomfortable months Denny and his family spent at Alki Point before moving across the bay, *Kwi-AHK-teed* paddled down the river with three of his sons to visit the American. He asked Denny to give his sons "Boston" names—*Boston* was the native term for *American*—and Denny selected those of three native chiefs famous in the Midwest: Keokuck, Tecumseh, and William.

Names were important to the Duwamish, who regarded special ones as heritable titles of distinction. As representatives of their respective peoples, *Kwi-AHK-teed* and Denny appear to have regarded the bestowal of names as a sign of friendship and a pledge of cooperation. This pledge served the settlers well, particularly during the hungry winter of 1852-1853 when they were able to buy 50 bushels of potatoes from the Duwamish. After *Kwi-AHK-teed* died, his sons and their people continued to maintain a friendship with the settlers, even after it was be-

Charley Keokuck, son of the famous Duwamish chief Kwi-AHK-teed, is shown here in 1904 with an unidentified child. Keokuck received his special "Boston" name from his father's friend Arthur Denny in the early 1850s. Courtesy, Special Collections Division, University of Washington Libraries

trayed during the time of the treaties.

As some pioneers hacked out townsites from the forests around the bay, others moved upriver. Early in 1853 Henry Tobin staked his claim on the Black River, and soon he had company. Dr. R.H. Bigelow discovered coal later that summer and took samples down to Seattle to test in a blacksmith's forge. Satisfied with their quality, Bigelow looked for backers to supplement his slender resources. Two, Obediah Eaton and Joseph Fanjoy, agreed to join him; with Henry Tobin they formed the Duwamish Coal Company on October 20.

Mines need timbers to shore up tunneling, and to provide a supply, Eaton, Fanjoy, and Tobin built a sawmill on the Black River. The mill appears to have been water powered, and in order to create a millrace and a holding pond, a six-foot-high log dam was built across the river. For assurance that the rising water would not exit from somewhere else on the lake, Fanjoy explored its shoreline—the first white man known to have done so—and returned a few days later to pronounce the dam watertight. In six weeks the water topped the dam, and by the beginning of 1854 the mill was in operation.

A brief description of this mill was left by George Gibbs, the man the new territorial governor, Isaac Stevens, had sent out to collect information about the native peoples. In January Gibbs visited the site and included this observation in his report.

A saw-mill was erected during the last autumn, upon the outlet of the lake, at a place where they [the Duwamish] are in the habit of taking salmon. The fishery was much improved by the dam, but what afforded the greatest satisfaction to them was its situation upon their property, and the superior importance thereby derived to themselves. They soon began to understand the machinery, and took every visitor through the building to explain its working, and boast of it as if it had been of their own construction.

The information Gibbs collected was intended to help Stevens in his efforts to draw up treaties with the area's native peoples. By 1853, when Washington Territory was created, there were 3,965 settlers in residence, but the land they claimed still belonged to native Americans. Treaties were the means by which the na-

RIGHT: Tecumseh, another son of Kwi-AHK-teed, proudly poses for his portrait, circa 1904. During his lifetime Tecumseh witnessed the arrival of the white settlers, conflicts between the two cultures, and the eventual disappearance of his tribe's traditional life-style. Courtesy, Special Collections Division, University of Washington Libraries

tive claim to the land could be abrogated, and in 1854 the governor and his staff were busy drawing up such documents.

The first treaty council, held on Medicine Creek south on the Sound in December, angered many native Americans, and by the time the second council was to take place at Point Elliott (Mukilteo), discontent was widespread. Fearing the loss of their homeland, the Duwamish balked at attending the council, but Governor Stevens prevailed, and on January 1, 1855, Keokuck signed the treaty.

Back home, the Duwamish were bitterly divided. Keokuck and his brothers sought to remain on friendly terms with the settlers in spite of the treaty, but others prepared to fight. Treaty councils east of the mountains produced their own share of discord, and by the summer the situation had become volatile. Complicating matters further, news of a gold strike in eastern Washington was sending heedless prospectors into the midst of a native population whose restlessness continued to mount.

Eaton and Fanjoy were among those who set out to try their luck in the gold fields. Neither the mine nor the mill had prospered as their backers had hoped. The Duwamish Coal Company had managed to send a schooner loaded with 300 tons of coal to San Francisco where it sold for $30 a ton, but this amount fell short of covering the debts the company had incurred. Adding to the company's problems was the failing health of partner Henry Tobin. When his wife Diana joined him in June 1855, Tobin was near death, and when he died a few months later she and her children were marooned in a wilderness on the eve of war.

Meanwhile, Eaton, Fanjoy, and several other prospectors headed into Yakima country with high hopes, but somewhere east of the Cascades they were killed by native warriors. Fears mounted. When the agent sent to apprehend the killers was himself slain, the army was called in, only to be repulsed in battle. This and the massacre of three families living on the White River inspired a wave of terror among the settlers, and most of them in King County fled to Seattle.

War plunged the region into chaos. In an attempt to divide native forces, officials sought to remove groups to temporary camps away from battle zones, but the policy only worsened an already wretched situation, and when the Duwamish were ordered to relocate down to the bay they refused. Those most closely related to the warring Yakima were readiest to fight, and *Elk-klah-kum* emerged as a prominent war leader. In December 1854 a band of Yakima and Wenatchee warriors crossed the mountains and camped on the east shore of Lake Washington, where they and their western allies planned a bold attack on Seattle.

On January 25, 1855, the term of enlistment for the volunteers posted at forts along the Duwamish expired, and they returned to Seattle. With them went Tecumseh, son of *Kwi-AHK-teed,* and a large number of Duwamish seeking protection. Taking advantage of the disappearance of the volunteers, the hostile force led by *Elk-klah-kum* and Yakima chief Qualchan crossed the lake on the morning of January 26, and attacked Seattle. Unable to seize the town after a day-long shoot-out, they returned to their stronghold, burning settlers' cabins and barns and the mill on the Black River as they retreated.

This failure to take Seattle heralded the end of the Indian War, and by October the army had allowed nearly 100 Duwamish to return to their home sites on the Black River. There they hastily erected smaller dwellings and set up their weirs. With the incipient white community now gone, the Duwamish sought to reconstruct their lives as previously. However, once the Treaty of Point Elliott was ratified by Congress in 1859, the land was no longer theirs; they thus found themselves at the mercy of new settlers who made their way up the river.

While no trace remains of the original Eaton, Fanjoy, and Tobin sawmill, this picture shows the first mill to be built near the south end of Lake Washington at Kennydale. Courtesy, Renton Historical Society and Museum

RIGHT: Erasmus M. Smithers gained a reputation as one of Renton's founding fathers, and not without reason. Homesteader, entrepreneur, businessman, and postmaster, he filed the first plat for the Town of Renton in 1875, and promoted the merits of being a Renton citizen. Courtesy, Renton Historical Society and Museum

By 1857, Eaton, Fanjoy, and Tobin were dead, and Bigelow had moved away, but their places were taken by others. The first of these newcomers was Erasmus M. Smithers, a young man from Virginia who left home at age 19 and came West in a wagon train. Once he arrived he hired himself out in lumber camps, and during the war he served in the territorial militia. In 1857 Smithers met and married Diana Tobin, who held the patent to her dead husband's donation claim. As impressed with the Black River area as Tobin had been, Smithers purchased a 160-acre claim adjoining his wife's, so that between them they owned nearly 480 acres of prime land.

In the 1860s new neighbors moved in. Christian Clymer and his wife Rachel took a claim on the west side of the Black River, and William Smith and Peter Andrews settled on the north bank of the Cedar. Native workers were hired to help with the backbreaking labor of clearing the land. To fell the huge trees, holes were bored in their trunks; fires were then lit and kept burning in their interiors until the giants toppled with a loud crash. In the shaded clearings gardens appeared, and the Smithers began a dairy.

The families were blessed with children, and Clymer built a schoolhouse on his claim. It was a rough little structure measuring about 14 feet by 16 feet, with hand-hewn plank floors and a mud-and-stone fireplace at one end. Mats woven by natives from cattails kept out chilling drafts. The children studied at handmade desks, and Peter Andrews' daughter Adelaide taught the occasional classes. On days when school was in session, the children on the east bank of the Black River crossed to the west over the Duwamish's tripod weirs.

It was a rustic, peaceful place, but change was in the wind. In 1862 rumors of coal in the area were confirmed by the discovery of seams near Issaquah Creek, south of Lake Sammamish. To extract the coal, a five-ton scow was poled and sailed on a route up the Duwamish and Black rivers, up Lake Washington and Sammamish River and Lake to Issaquah Creek, where the coal was stockpiled—in all, a roundtrip journey of 140 miles, taking 20 days to complete.

This was only the beginning, however. In 1865 new seams were discovered in the hills east of Lake Washington, and the Black River settlers looked on eagerly as barges began regular trips into the lake. The settlers' homesteads served as handy stopping places where meals, lodging, and supplies could be obtained while native crews visited nearby kin.

The growing importance of the little settlement was noted in

The Claus Jorgenson family came to Renton after establishing a homestead on the Duwamish River. This photo of their homestead was probably taken in the 1880s. Courtesy, Renton Historical Society and Museum

January 1867, when Christian Clymer was appointed postmaster and his home became the Black River Post Office, a vital way station on the mail route from Seattle to Ranger's Prairie in the upper Snoqualmie valley. Later that year the route was improved with the construction of a bridge—which became known as Black Bridge—over the Black River, at a place just north of the present intersection of South Third Street and Rainier Avenue. Eventually the road was extended to Snoqualmie Pass and became the major overland route to the interior.

Nevertheless, rivers remained the major arteries of travel. On the Black River steam tugs made their appearance, chuffing along at the lead of coal barges. The increasing activity of these vessels led a number of Black River settlers to petition the government for the removal of the remaining Duwamish to reservations so that their fishweirs would no longer obstruct traffic on the waterway. A countermovement led by Arthur Denny and Henry Yesler (both of whom had invested heavily in a tramway that competed with river traffic) succeeded in sidetracking the petition.

By 1871 coal from the new mining center of Newcastle was being barged across Lake Washington to the Lake Union portage, and from that lake's south shore to Elliott Bay. On its way from the mine mouth to the bay, the coal had to be loaded and unloaded 11 times; nevertheless, it beat the Black River route, where traffic eventually slowed to a trickle.

This rerouting dealt a blow to the Black River settlers, though they were still able to profit from Newcastle's boom by supplying its population with produce from their farms. By 1871 families along the river could count at least a dozen children, and a larger one-room schoolhouse was built near what is now the intersection of Fourth and Main. Although this growth was slight, in the back of settlers' minds remained the recollection of Bigelow's earlier discovery of coal, and when they were not tending to their farms they went in search of the elusive seam.

Erasmus Smithers diligently explored streams where there was float coal—chunks lying loose in the beds. Out hunting one day in May 1873, he followed a trail of float up a streambed until it disappeared. With his pick he struck the bank at that point and almost immediately uncovered a thick black seam. On this adventure Smithers was accompanied by a man named Crane and, according to the Duwamish, James Moses, known locally as "Jimmy Moses," the grandson of *Tee-LAH-sah,* a headman at *Tu-hu-DEE-du.* The Duwamish had known about coal, the "rock that burns," but had had no great use for it. Leave it to the white man to value something that smelled bad when it burned!

Like those who formed the Duwamish Coal Company, Smithers was short on develop-

In 1893 Newcastle was touted as a premier coal mining center of the West. The vastness of the mining operations, and the tidiness of the village, not to mention the quaint church and schoolhouse, idealized what was in reality a tightly controlled company town. Courtesy, Renton Historical Society and Museum

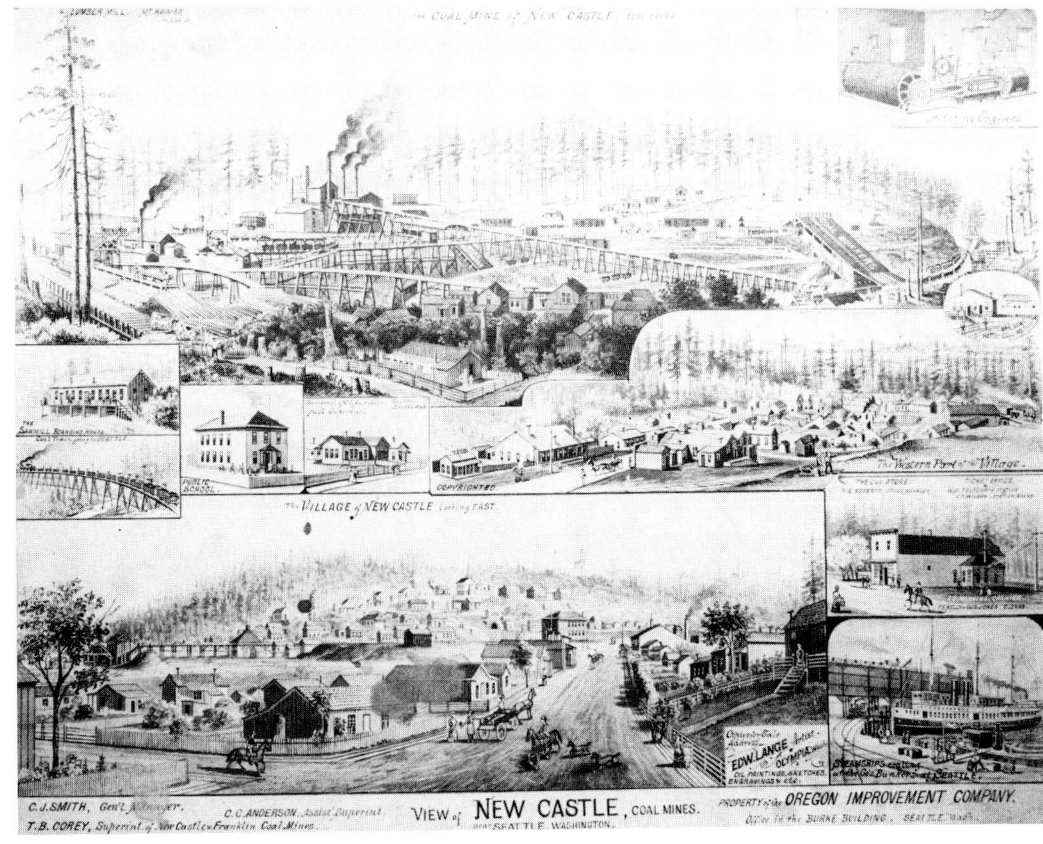

ABOVE: Captain William Renton envisioned many possibilities in the burgeoning Northwest. Local business investments centering around the extraction, transportation, and processing of coal and timber helped to create his fortune. Courtesy, Renton Historical Society and Museum

RIGHT: The Reverend George F. Whitworth influenced both economic and spiritual development in Renton, and later went on to become president of the Territorial University of Washington. Courtesy, Special Collections Division, University of Washington Libraries

ment capital, but monied backers were quick to come forward. In fact, Smithers could not have discovered the coal at a better time.

Barely two months after Smithers went public with his find, the town of Seattle learned that the Northern Pacific Railroad had selected Commencement Bay rather than Elliott Bay as the terminus of the transcontinental route. Stunned by the news, town leaders bravely announced their intention to construct a transcontinental railroad of their own.

Organized as the Seattle and Walla Walla Railroad (S&WW), its backers planned to lay track around the southern end of Lake Washington and over Snoqualmie Pass to Walla Walla where, fortune permitting, it would join track with some other line. They understood, however, that investors were not likely to lay their money down on such a long shot. So it was decided to build the road in smaller, more easily financed stages to places where it would pay to transport something like timber—or coal.

A trustee of the S&WW who had such a plan in mind was Captain William Renton, a rumpled bear of a man who in 1873 was one of the most successful businessmen in the territory. Born in Pictou, a seaport in Nova Scotia, Renton began a life at sea at age 11. Skill in mathematics led him into the ranks of ship's officer at 18, and by 25 he was master of his own vessel. A shrewdly intelligent man, Renton arrived in San Francisco in 1850 and realized quickly that fortunes awaited those who could satisfy that city's ravenous appetites, especially for lumber, as it was in the habit of burning itself down every few years. Loading sawmill machinery onto a ship, Renton and several associates sailed north to Puget Sound where, song had it, timber grew "thick as hair on the back of a dog." After a few false starts, Renton settled at Port Blakely, near George Vancouver's landing site on Bainbridge Island, and built what became the largest lumber mill on the continent.

By the 1870s Renton and his partners were looking for profitable ways to invest their fortunes, and an independent railroad heading into huge stands of virgin timber looked like a pretty good prospect. The deal was sweetened by the fact that Smithers' coal mine was several miles closer to Seattle than the Newcastle mines and right on the route surveyed by Thomas Morris, the engineer hired by the railroad. With Renton's financial backing, Smithers, Morris, and Charles Shattuck, president of the Seattle Coal Company, the organization running the Newcastle mines, organized the Renton Coal Company.

Once the deposits were surveyed and found workable, the Renton Coal Company's manager, Ruel Robinson, purchased the mine from Smithers and other nearby land owners. On March 25, 1874, the company was incorporated with a capital stock of 30,000 shares at $100 each. To encourage local stock purchases, company officer Charles Burnett was authorized to offer shares for $50 and the option of buying coal from the mine for $4 a ton—half the normal rate.

Six months later another coal seam—an extension of Smithers' discovery—was uncovered about a mile southeast of the Smithers mine, and another company, the Talbot Company, was organized to develop the new site. Like those of the Renton Company, many of Talbot's officers and trustees, such as John Leary, James McNaught, and Seattle mayor John Collins, were heavily involved in the S&WW.

With money and strong management the mines boomed. Workers picked and blasted tunnels into the rock, erected hoists, and constructed huge bunkers to hold the coal. A tramway from the bunkers was built to deliver the coal to barges on the Black River. The Renton Company had the steam tug *Addie* and several 80-foot-long barges built at Hammond's shipyard in Seattle in order to haul coal. Cannon boomed and steam whistles blew as the *Addie* slid down the ways, and it was soon busy bringing the Renton Company's coal to the bunkers built on Yesler's wharf. To transport its coal to its bunkers, the Talbot Company brought the steam tug *Wenat* up from the Columbia River.

Within a year the Black River area was transformed from a rural farming community into a bustling mining center. To provide shoring timbers and lumber for the buildings rising in the valley, lumberman David Parker and his sons Leroy and James set up their sawmill near what is now the intersection of Third and Mill streets. With deafening crashes the big trees were felled and sweating millmen fed the ponderous trunks to the screaming saws.

In an atmosphere heady with coal smoke and sawdust, Smithers and the other officers of the Renton Coal Company considered the time ripe to plat a town and offer lots for sale. On September 4, 1875, Smithers in association with Morris and Shattuck filed a plat with the county auditor in Seattle. The town boundaries ran south from the Cedar River along Burnett Street three-quarters of a mile to Seventh Avenue, east five blocks to Cedar Street, and north back to the river.

To honor its financial patron, the town was named Renton. Across its rectangular grid ran the diagonal slash of Walla Walla Avenue, the hopeful portal of Seattle's embryonic transcontinental railroad.

Building a railroad, however, even in short sections, was easier dreamed than done. Even by the time Renton was platted, two years after Seattle's citizens had inaugurated construction at a spirited May Day picnic, not an inch of track had actually been laid along the route, even with a $100,000 loan from Captain Renton.

Work on the project continued, however. The Renton and Talbot companies extended their tramway from the mines to Steele's Landing, a more convenient place to load barges. In 1876 Chinese crews finished grading the roadbed from the mouth of the Duwamish to Steele's Landing. Next, trestles and bridges were built, ties were laid, and on September 25, crews began spiking down the first rails.

Finally, by February 1877, the narrow-gauge track reached Renton, and on March 17 a shiny new locomotive, the *A.A. Denny,* steamed out of the depot at the foot of Seattle's Second Avenue, pulling a coach and four flatcars with 250 jubilant citizens. Trailing a thick pall of smoke, the train huffed across the trestle above the tideflats and disappeared up the Duwamish valley.

Alongside the river, settlers cheered from their yards as the train rolled by. One hour out, it reached Steele's Landing and headed east, then north, to Renton, the first town tied to Seattle with bands of steel. Crossing the Black River, it entered a clearing where onlookers, gathered in front of rough-cut buildings, announced their town. Above rose the hills, ragged with timber and heavy with coal. At the end of the line, the train hissed to a stop before the depot, amid a cloud of steam and a chorus of cheers that swelled the air.

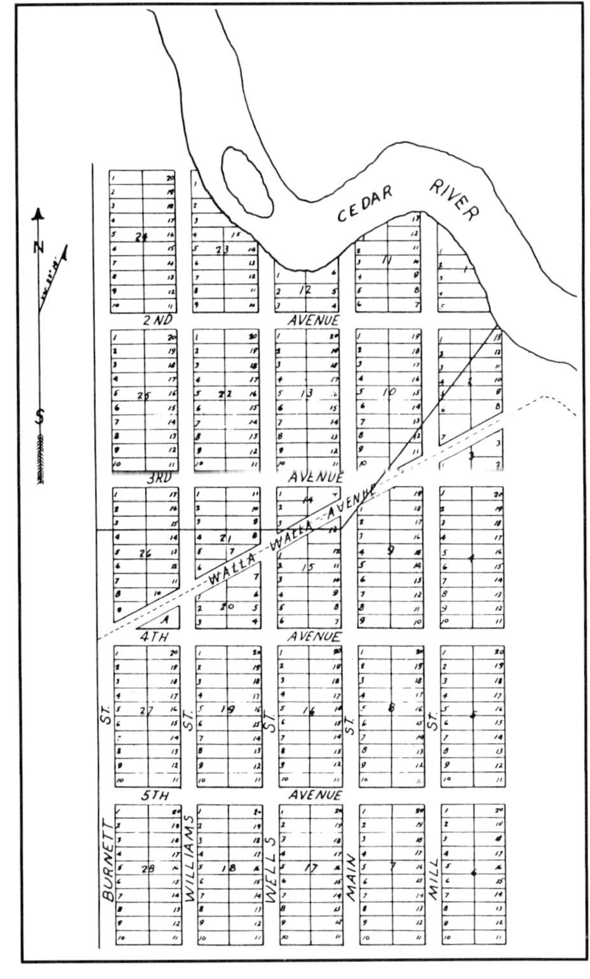

The town plat for Renton was filed by Erasmus Smithers on September 4, 1875. Note the Cedar River and the diagonal cut of Walla Walla Avenue. Courtesy, Renton Historical Society and Museum

CHAPTER 3

A Tide of Growth

The Renton Volunteer Fire Department poses with its water hose cart in front of its new fire station on Wells Street, circa 1908. Aside from the vital service of fire fighting, the department also worked to bring a sense of spirit to Renton through community and athletic events. The Volunteer Fire Department's commitment to the community is evident in the fact that the city did not have to hire its first paid firefighter until 1944. Courtesy, Renton Historical Society and Museum

The train depot at the foot of Mill Street was a crude structure supported by two huge fir stumps. Surrounding it lay a raw landscape of stumps, mud, and a few board buildings. Renton looked very much the wild West town, and it had a reputation to match.

Barely three weeks before the *A.A. Denny* arrived, a young man named John Thompson had tried to stab someone in a drunken brawl that had started in Agnew's Saloon on Walla Walla Avenue. The combatants stumbled out to the tracks where a bystander, Solomon Baxter, tried to intervene and got Thompson's knife in his stomach for his trouble.

This happened on a Sunday. On Monday Baxter died. On Tuesday Thompson was arraigned in court, and the case was put before a jury on Thursday. On Friday Thompson was found

RIGHT: The coal mining that played a major role in Renton's early industry held many dangers and risks for the miners, who worked 10-hour days, collecting less than 30 cents an hour. Later, union labor strikes would shake the coal mining industry, severely impacting the companies, as well as miners and their families. Courtesy, Renton Historical Society and Museum

guilty, and on Saturday he was sentenced to hang. The speed of justice in this case was cause for considerable self-congratulation, and when Thompson was hanged in September, he had the dubious honor of being the first man lawfully hanged in King County and the first white man hanged in the Territory.

At the time, the town stretched from the mines to the river like knots on a rope. Miners' shacks clustered around the Renton mine entrance on the north side of Renton Hill. On the townsite itself David Parker ran a boarding house near his mill, and stores had been recently opened by George Tibbetts and H.H. Snow. There was also a blacksmith shop as well as several saloons, including the infamous Agnew's. Additionally, Smithers and others who had purchased lots built housing for workers and their families.

On the brow of the hill south of Renton stood the community of Talbot, which had grown up in picturesquely haphazard fashion around the entrance of that mine. In a July 25, 1877, article in the *Daily Pacific Tribune,* a writer described the view from the top of Talbot Hill:

The town and the works of the Company are wide spread, or rather much separated, the bunkers and shipping point being at the end of the railroad, the opening of the main tunnel all by itself a half mile distant, the camp of the Chinese between the town, the town of the single men and saloon a quarter of a mile beyond the tunnel, and the store, boarding house, blacksmith shop and town of the families a half mile over the hill in another direction, and near the mouth of the first tunnel. No two of the town's divisions are in sight of each other, while if all were together it would be quite a place.

Exhaustive work under difficult conditions did not prevent Renton miners from seeing the lighter side of life. Here, two miners use a "Donkey Telephone," while the mule caught in the middle waits for the joke to end. Mules played an important role in the early mines, hauling the heavily laden coal cars. Courtesy, Renton Historical Society and Museum

At that time the attention of most citizens of Renton was focused on extracting coal from the ground. In the beginning workers at the Renton mine dug a level tunnel into the highest of three coal seams south for a distance of nearly 1,500 feet. Later a shaft known as a slope was blasted through overlaying rock to the second seam and followed its 12-degree decline into the earth for over a mile. Tracks were laid in the slope, and a hoist built at the entrance lowered cars into the mine and lifted them out.

The most common method of mining coal in King County was to bore tunnels called gangways into the coal seam at right angles from the slope. Several hundred feet normally

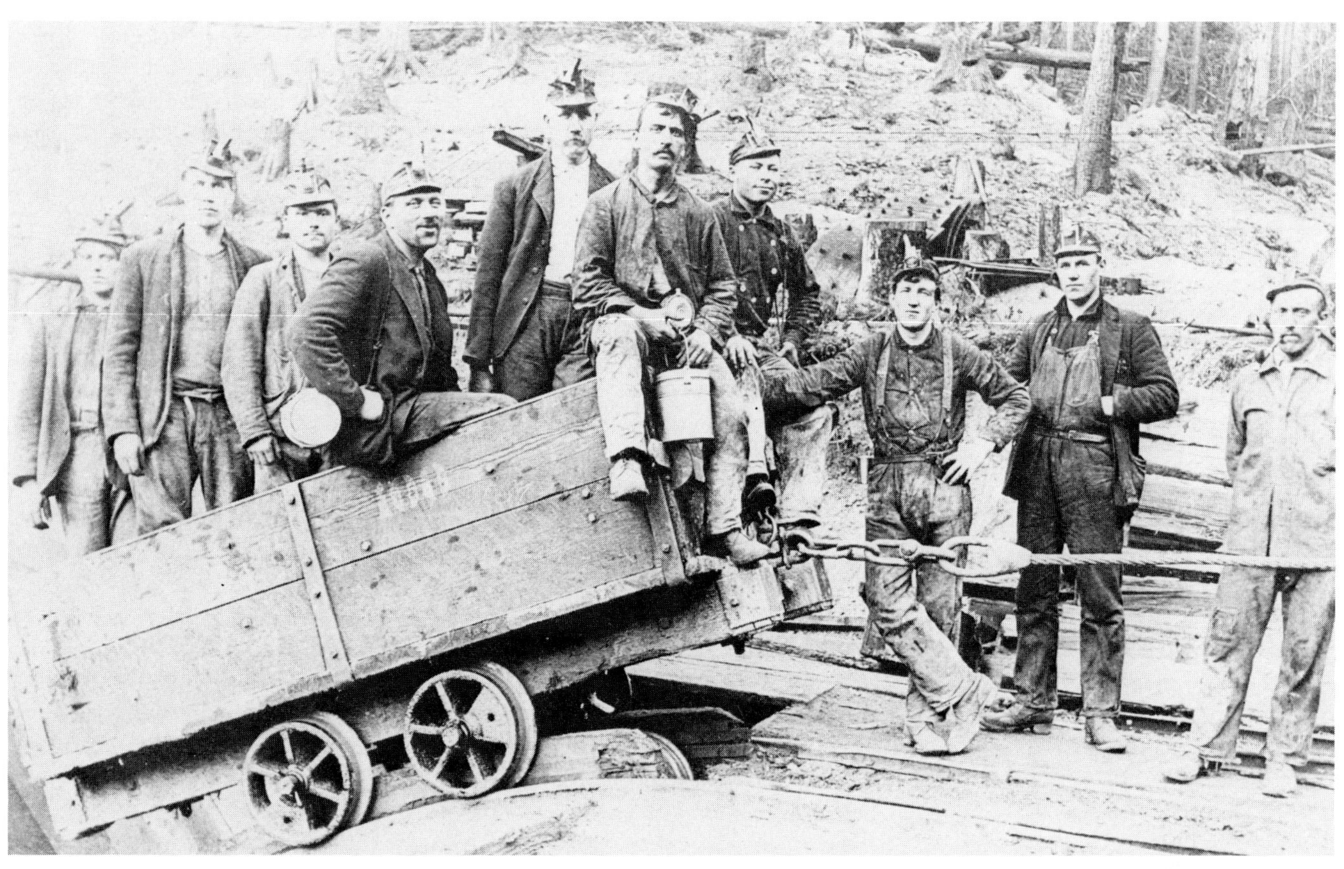

separated one gangway from another, and the coal between them was mined out in a series of chutes 8 to 12 feet wide, dug at more or less right angles from the gangway and separated one from another by 40 to 90 feet of coal. The intervening coal bodies, called pillars, were pierced by shafts and crosscuts that allowed air to circulate. Depending on the strength of the roof, a chute might be widened, forming what was called a breast or room.

Eventually this system of gangways, chutes, breasts, and crosscuts resembled an enormous subterranean lattice. Ultimately 22 gangways penetrated the second and the third, richer seam of coal at the Renton mine roughly every 300 feet along the main slope.

The coal was dug by hand with picks and shovels in low tunnels where the air was rank and often thick with coal dust. Before electricity came to the mine, the only available light was from lanterns hung from timbers or from lamps on the miners' hats, which burned oil and later carbide. Cars in the gangways were hauled by mules to the slope where they were then joined together and hauled to the entrance by the hoist.

The work was hard, dirty, and dangerous. Cave-ins were a constant threat along with gas explosions. Gas emitted from the coal was drawn off by huge fans, though enough could still collect to be dangerous; in fact miners welcomed the appearance of rats in the tunnels as a sign the air was safe. When the rats left the miners were quick to follow!

Once out of the mine, the coal was cleaned of waste material and graded according to size by screens. Loaded into bunkers that each held a thousand tons, the coal awaited transport by railroad cars to loading docks on Elliott Bay.

The rhythm of life in the mines was dictated by the whistle that announced the change in 10-hour shifts. In the early afternoon men and boys walked from the town to the mine entrance in clean clothes and shiny hats, each carrying a deep lunch pail. The whistle blew, and the hoist halted so that the departing shift underground could climb aboard a train of cars and be brought to the surface. A troop of weary miners black with dust, their headlamps

The clean faces and hands of these miners indicate that they are just beginning their daily shift at the Newcastle Mine. Courtesy, Renton Historical Society and Museum

still burning, thus traded places with the new shift that was lowered on the rumbling train deep into the mine.

Above ground there was plenty of work to be had in the lumber trade. Before large-scale logging got underway in the 1880s, farmers along the Black and Cedar rivers often simply burned the trees they cut down. Lumber produced by large mills was cheap enough so that small mill owners barely survived on the thinnest of profit margins, and trees were cut primarily to open land for agriculture. Eventually, though, as more people moved in and the mines were developed, logging began to pay.

On the highlands above the Cedar River, logs were sometimes transported down long flumes. From fall to spring, rafts of logs and shingle bolts—cut sections of cedar from which shingles were fashioned—were docked along the river bank. During the spring flood, native men and others familiar with the river guided the rafts down to the mills. The first shingle mill in the Renton area was operated by Captain Robert Brown on the north side of the Cedar River. Here, shingles and shakes were split, cut, and trimmed by hand, and then later by saws powered by water flowing off Sartori Hill.

Gradually, by dint of enormous labor,

An important industry in early Renton history, logging in and around Renton created jobs, cleared extensive areas of land, and provided timber for new homes and businesses. The logs in this 1896 photograph were being transported from the May Creek area by railroad cars, which could disconnect and adjust to the needed space between the different lengths of logs. Courtesy, Renton Historical Society and Museum

Trees were cut high above the ground to avoid the flaring, pitch-laden trunk, and fallers balancing on springboards swung double-bitted axes and push-pulled long "misery-ships" to topple the giants. At the cry of "Timber!" the men jumped for their lives to avoid the massive, flailing trunk. Once down, the tree was cut into various lengths and hauled by oxen down skidroads—trails set with half-buried logs—to the mill or river. To ease the logs' groaning passage, a "greaser" swabbed the skids with noisome dogfish oil while the "bull of the woods" atop the logs urged his oxen on with judicious use of a bull whip and liberal doses of profanity.

the shaggy forests were chopped back. After the Northern Pacific Railroad was completed in 1883, immigration into Washington Territory increased dramatically.

Nevertheless, growth in Renton was slow. The census of 1880 counted some 400 people in and around the town; however, in 1890 Renton's population was only 409. Nationally and regionally, the 1880s were difficult years economically, especially in extractive industries like coal and lumber. In 1886 the Renton-Talbot mine—joined physically and corporately—closed. Prone to flooding, the old north tunnel was abandoned and workers who lived near its entrance moved into town. Economic doldrums were punctuated by worker unrest culminating in riots that drove the Chinese from the area in 1885-1886. Yet the town insisted upon surviving.

Renton's few businesses clustered along or near Walla Walla Avenue, next to the tracks. In 1877 H.H. Snow's store stood on Mill Street between Second and Third. James Tonkin's false-fronted merchandise store was on the triangle of land formed by the intersection of Walla Walla, Fourth, and Williams, presently the site of Tonkin Park. Robert Wood's department store, staffed by his large family, could be found on the corner of Walla Walla and Main, near Charles Custer's hardware store and Mrs. May Kline's Renton Hotel, the first rooming house in town.

It was in these commercial establishments that Renton's future was born. The stores sold groceries, meat, clothing, tools, and virtualy everything else needed for life in a developing land. Beside supplying residents in town, the stores also served those who traveled by canoe over river and lake or by horse and wagon over trails or rutted county roads from the coal camps and isolated farmsteads. Coal towns like Newcastle, Ravensdale, Kangley, or Black Diamond might boom while demand for coal was high, but Renton's slower, steadier growth and its more diverse economy enabled it to flourish when these other towns subsided into obscurity or disappeared altogether.

Cheek by jowl with the stores and shops were Renton's saloons, nine of them by 1885. They catered primarily to single, working men who left the mines, mills, and logging camps for town to have some fun on Saturday night and to stock up on supplies on Sunday, their one day off. Saloons offered camaraderie and a chance to catch up on the news as well as music, drink, and the company of bar girls.

Not all of Renton's populace was happy with the sometimes violent goings-on of the saloon crowd, and the spectacle of the sabbath spent in dalliance positively horrified the Reverend George Whitworth. In a long and busy career beginning in 1853, Whitworth, who was called the father of Presbyterianism in Washington, founded at least 20 churches. Among them was Renton's first, First Presbyterian, organized in David Parker's home on December 13,

The immense size of the old growth timber harvested in the Renton area is illustrated by this 1907 shipment of fir. The capacity of each railcar was equal to just one of these enormous logs. Courtesy, Renton Historical Society and Museum

One of the first store owners in Renton, Harmon Hartman Snow opened a combination general store and hotel under the name of Snows Hotel in 1876. The store was located on Mill Street between Second and Third, and in 1879 Snow took on the additional duties of postmaster. This portrait of Snow was taken in 1886. Courtesy, Renton Historical Society and Museum

1885. Parker, his wife Emmaline, and four other pioneer wives were the church's members, and with help from the Presbyterian Board of Missions, they succeeded in putting up a white frame building, complete with steeple and bell, overlooking the town on Mill Avenue.

A church was one sign of civic stability; a school was another, and in Renton these stood close together. The 1871 schoolhouse had been replaced by a larger building, but by 1876, with 82 school-age children in town, an even larger building was constructed at the corner of Wells and Walla Walla. By the 1890s this facility also proved too small, and an elegant two-story, four-room building with a concrete foundation and a bell tower was built on Fifth Avenue between Wells and Main streets. This was called the Central School, and in its first year 110 students attended classes.

It was no accident that the church and school were built on the slope of the hill. Only 10 feet above sea level, most of Renton was flooded when the rivers overran their banks. Jack Hayes recalled the difficulty of getting around in the early days.

In the winter when you took your girl visiting, a lantern was just as important as the girl. You both had to be somewhat of an athlete to jump from one duck board to another and one rock to a hummock of dry ground. If you missed, well, you went back home to put on dry socks unless you had your gum boots on.

In the winter (whenever they were not buried underwater) the town's streets were often churned into mire, and in the summer they were thick with dust. After the road from Seattle over Black Bridge to Snoqualmie Pass was opened in 1867, cattlemen east of the mountains began to use it to drive their herds to slaughterhouses in Seattle. In the 1870s and 1880s, during the fall, Renton citizens often had to vacate their streets as herds of longhorns milled through town, spurred on by native cowboys who charged up and down the line on their cayuse ponies.

But however wild and woolly Renton might have been in the early days, as more railroads were built it quickly became a significant commercial and transportation hub. In 1878 the S&WW extended its tracks to Newcastle, and tonnage on the road increased dramatically. In 1880 New York financier Henry Villard purchased both the mines and the railroad, renaming it the Columbia and Puget Sound (C&PS).

Villard's purchase was part of his larger strategy to dominate the Northern Pacific (NP). To this end, in 1881 he became president of the NP's Board of Directors and completed the NP transcontinental route in 1883. Part of his ambitious plans to dominate Northwestern transportation involved building a branch line up the Cedar River to a promising new coal field prospected in 1880 by a mining engineer from California's Black Diamond Coal Company. Construction on the line began; however, Villard's personal ambitions exceeded his capacity to realize them, and within a few years he filed for bankruptcy.

Meanwhile, work on the Cedar River extension dawdled along; nevertheless, by 1884 its narrow-gauge tracks had reached the new Black Diamond mine, and coal began to move down the tracks. In that same year, the tracks from Renton were linked with those of the NP, and at long last Seattle—and Renton—had transcontinental connections.

By 1887 the narrow-gauge tracks of the C&PS had been replaced by standard gauge, and later the completion of the Lake Washington Belt Line along the lake's eastern shore put Renton in touch with the booming coal district at Gillman (Issaquah). In 1896 the Seattle and Rainier Beach Railway (S&RB), an electric streetcar line beginning in Seattle, reached Main Street in Renton. Stretching 12 miles in length, it was the longest electric railway in the state at the time and one of the longest in the world.

David and Emmaline Parker came to Renton in the early 1870s, and with their two sons built and operated a sawmill at Third and Mill. The Parkers were very involved in Renton community affairs, and played a pivotal role in establishing the town's first church. Courtesy, Renton Historical Society and Museum

When the Central School was completed in 1892, there was serious concern that the building was much too large to ever be filled by children from the surrounding district. Eight years later, however, Renton's first high school class graduated from this school. Courtesy, Renton Historical Society and Museum

The Northern Pacific railroad depot in Renton, pictured here in 1912, was located at Fifth and Burnett. Note the trunks which were commonly used for travel at that time. Courtesy, Renton Historical Society and Museum

RIGHT: The Seattle & Renton Railway, shown here in 1895, carried workers, tourists, and families up to Seattle for a day of adventure. Courtesy, Renton Historical Society and Museum, Howard Hill Collection

The advent of the S&RB introduced Renton to a new technology. The first electric light introduced in King County was the one that burned aboard the steamer *Willamette* when it docked in Seattle in 1881. By 1889 the Seattle Electric Company had completed the world's first underground hydroelectric generating facility at Snoqualmie Falls. A year later the power from its generators was sent to Seattle via a substation built at Third and Mill in Renton, the town's first brick building, which today houses the Renton area Multi Service Center. Although at the time most of the power went to running the S&RB, eventually it electrified the mines.

Improvements in transportation fueled growth, and by 1900 Renton's population had reached 1,176, a nearly four-fold increase in 10 years. Growth was also spurred by the 1895 reopening of the Renton-Talbot mine by the local Renton Cooperative Company. Compared with the output of other mines in the area, the Cooperative Company's tonnages were small—only 2,420 tons in 1885—but they increased dramatically in 1901 when the venture was purchased by the Seattle Electric Company, which made major improvements.

In that same year a new industry located in Renton. While scouting the area for new investment opportunities, two California entrepreneurs, James Doyle and J.R. Miller, discovered that the shale overlaying the Renton mine's coal seams produced a high quality clay. Tests indicated the material would make excellent brick, and in association with a Seattle investor, E.J. Mathews, the men organized the Renton Clay Works and began to develop a plant on the south bank of the Cedar River. The market for brick, particularly the kind used to pave streets, ballooned as Western states entered a period of rapid urban growth, and the plant at Renton eventually became the largest producer of paving brick in the world.

For Renton 1901 was a banner year. On September 6 it was incorporated as a fourth-class town, with a local doctor, Abijah Ives Beach, as its first mayor. In this first year the town collected $344.50, some of it from the sale of dog tags and a horse license, but most—$300—from licensing a wholesale liquor distributor. The town council wrestled with problems such as railroad cars blocking streets and what to do with free-roaming cows. Council members attempted to control the latter problem by requiring licenses for cows living within the town limits, but since a cow with a license was just as much of a problem as one without, they eventually decided to banish the animals from town altogether.

When it was not banning cattle, the council worked hard to bring about civic improvements by, for example, creating a municipal water supply. The first water system in Renton was developed in 1882 by Norman Davis: water from the Cedar River was pumped into a tank and then piped to a few nearby homes via wood mains made from hand-bored logs. The system was small, however, and proved to be of little use when the town nearly burned down in 1899.

This occurred one blustery day when sparks from a passing train started a fire on Walla Walla Avenue along a block of houses called Brannon's Row. Most of Renton's male population was in Seattle at the time, attending a Cooperative Coal Company meeting.

An eyewitness rushed to inform them of the fire by means of a telephone that had just been installed in Thomas Harries' grocery store. It was a long distance call, and the concerned citizen making it, unfamiliar with the new invention, wanted to be sure his voice carried. When he bellowed "Renton is on fire!" at the top of his lungs into the mouthpiece, the sound of his voice filled the entire hall on the other end of the line.

Immediately the men hopped a train back to town; in the meantime, Renton's women had succeeded in forming a bucket brigade. Although Brannon's Row burnt to the ground, the brigade's efforts with the buckets and wet blankets commandeered from Tonkin's store had saved adjacent structures.

Two positive results from this near-catastrophe were the organization of Renton's volunteer fire department in 1901 and the creation of a municipal water supply. Crystal Spring, which generated 90,000 gallons of pure water a day on the north slope of Renton Hill, was tapped: a headworks dam was built, and a snaking wooden main channeled the water from the spring down to a wooden storage tank where other mains distributed it to businesses and homes. In 1909 a larger supply was brought to town from Springbrook Creek.

As it developed its water supply, the town also started a sewer system. The honor of installing the town's first septic tank went to James Tachell, its first undertaker and livery stable owner, who built the first sewer connection with a septic tank sometime after 1903. After 1910 the city began sewer construction, in the words of its utility department, with the "gradual and spasmodic" replacement of septic tanks with sewer mains.

The more the region developed, the more favorable Renton's location appeared. In 1902 the Seattle-Tacoma Interurban Railroad commenced service through the Duwamish and White river valleys, providing what was remembered as the best rail service Renton ever had. In 1906 the Chicago, Milwaukee, and St. Paul Railroad obtained the right of way on the C&PS tracks from Seattle to Maple Valley; and when the Milwaukee Road, as it was called, was completed in 1910, Renton had its second transcontinental rail connection.

By that time Renton was linked by steel rails to a broad hinterland. The coal of Newcas-

This early 1900s view of the clay beds at the Denny-Renton Clay and Coal Company shows how the earth was broken away from the cliff faces with the use of hydraulic power. Courtesy, Renton Historical Society and Museum

RIGHT: Dr. Abijah I. Beach served as the first mayor of Renton. He and his wife (center couple) lived in this residence located at the corner of 4th and Wells. Dr. Beach first came to Renton as the company doctor of the Renton Coal Company, and later moved into private practice and then into politics. Courtesy, Renton Historical Society and Museum

tle, Black Diamond, and a host of other mines rumbled through town, and families in outlying communities made regular trips to Renton for supplies.

Although overshadowed by rail connections, the river and lakes continued to serve as arteries of commerce and travel; on Lake Washington Renton emerged as a major freshwater port. Additionally, the construction of roads enabled Renton to service an expanding agricultural area as farmers cultivated more and more of the rich valley bottom soil.

As the town grew so did its number of social institutions. By 1901 the First Presbyterian Church had been joined by St. Luke's Episcopal Church and the First Baptist Church. In 1902 the United Methodist Church was organized, followed four years later by St. Anthony's Catholic Church. In 1907 the four-room Sartori School was built north of town, and two years later a one-room schoolhouse was constructed across the Black River in Earlington. In addition, the town had a succession of newspapers: the short-lived *Renton Argus* in 1906, the *Renton Journal* from 1909 to 1910, and later the *Renton*

The water reservoir on Talbot Hill was built in 1910, adding to Renton's increasing system of waterworks. In 1909, the town of Renton was paying $160 a month in water bills to the city of Seattle. Courtesy, Renton Historical Society and Museum

In 1911, Third Street was still dirt and mud, but it had railroad tracks down its center, an important sign of economic growth for a developing town. Courtesy, Renton Historical Society and Museum

Herald. In 1909 the town's first bank, Citizen's Bank, opened for business in a brick building at Fourth and Wells.

Renton was indeed becoming a more civilized place, although in 1901 the beleaguered city council was pressed to pass another ordinance banning horses along with the dreaded cows from the town's sidewalks. In 1910 the census counted 2,740 residents; North Renton had been annexed; a bandstand was erected beside the new city hall; and homes surrounded by neat picket fences marched in ranks up Renton Hill against a retreating ridgeline of uncut timber.

In that same year the Renton Chamber of Commerce printed a glowing descripton of their community, *Renton, The Town of Payrolls.* Besides the coal mine and the brick factory, now run by the Denny-Renton Clay and Coal Company, the town was also the site of entrepreneur William Pigott's Seattle Car Manufacturing Company. Besides excellent rail connections, Renton also offered the company space to expand, and by 1910 its shops north of town were turning out three to four railroad cars a day to serve expanding rail networks in the United States, Alaska, and China.

There was also a bottle factory, an ice plant, a plant that produced coal briquettes, two lumber companies, and a shingle mill. Together these industries provided a diverse economic base for what was still a small town, and the payrolls they generated supported an equally diverse commercial and service community that had expanded beyond Walla Walla Avenue to Third. In a little over 30 years, Renton had grown from a coal mine in a clearing to the second major industrial center of the county. Yet, great as these developments were, they merely hinted at things to come.

The site Henry Tobin had claimed with high hopes had indeed exceeded expectations, with one singular exception: it was prone to flooding. Low elevation meant that tidal influence ranged as far inland as the mouth of the Black River, where horse clams could be dug out of the mud. When the White and Cedar rivers flooded, their runoff often caused the Black River to reverse course and flow into the lake, a phenomenon that led the native people to name it Mox La Push, in Chinook jargon, "the river with two mouths."

The area's complex stream pattern often prolonged the flooding. Logging and land clearing had removed much of the vegetation that impeded outflow, and the dredging of river

RIGHT: Civic-minded Ignazio Sartori donated portions of his land for the Sartori School and the Renton Carnegie Library. Courtesy, Renton Historical Society and Museum

channels improved drainage somewhat, but floods continued to plague the town. In 1907 high water on the Cedar River quenched the kilns at the brick factory, and during the winter of 1910-1911, backflow from the White River turned Renton into a lake.

Reduced lowland flooding was thus one of the advantages of a plan to turn Lake Washington into a freshwater port by connecting it to Puget Sound via a canal. Since the average level of the lake surface was nearly 20 feet above the mean water level of the Sound, lowering the lake level would enable the lake's entrant streams to drain more efficiently.

The idea of a canal had first been broached by Thomas Mercer in 1854, but location had become cause for debate. Those who lived beside the Black River proposed simply dredging the Duwamish and Black rivers; however, besides running counter to the interests of Seattle investors, army engineers determined this scheme to be impractical.

Instead, Mercer's original plan for a canal from Salmon Bay through Lake Union to Lake Washington was followed. Lake Washington would be lowered to the level of Lake Union, the levels of both bodies of water to be regulated by locks and a dam at the narrows of Salmon Bay. The lowering of Lake Washington would effectively choke off the Black River, so that waters emptying into the lake would enter the Sound through the canal.

After the plan was accepted, Renton's city council organized a waterway district to manage construction of a new channel that would redirect the Cedar River into the lake. Once this channel was completed, the Black River would cease to exist.

Almost as if to mock efforts to constrain it, the Cedar River went on a record-breaking rampage in November 1911. It had been a rainy fall, and in the mountains a warm Chinook wind melted the snowpack, swelling the flood. Up at Cedar Lake, in an attempt to hold back the overflow, workmen added a wooden superstructure to the timber dam that

Spacious lots, a grand view of the lake and valley, and neat picket fences illustrate the benefits of living on Renton Hill at the turn of the century. The homes of Renton Hill were built with craftsmanship and grace, which distinguished the hill with a sense of elegance. Courtesy, Renton Historical Society and Museum

In its 1913 catalogue the Seattle Car and Foundry, now known as PACCAR Inc, proudly portrayed the layout of its Renton plant. Courtesy, PACCAR Inc

the municipality of Seattle had built to generate electricity. When their work showed signs of collapse, warning was sent downriver, and plans were set in motion to evacuate Renton: Once failure appeared imminent, the siren at the Renton mine would sound and alert residents to quickly gather their valuables and provisions and head for higher ground.

By November 18 the Cedar had risen above its banks, and near its mouth it spanned the floodplain. Muddy, full of drift, and wickedly turbulent, it clawed at its banks and threatened the foundation of the railroad bridge. To steady the structure, a locomotive moved back and forth along its length. That evening, in the pouring rain, people began to evacuate their homes.

On the morning of November 19 the wooden superstructure on the dam gave way, and a wall of water swept down the valley. At 6:30 P.M. the siren blew. "Its shriek," recalled Frank Storey, "could run up and down five octaves and raise the hair on the back of your neck."

In near panic, people raced for safety. Mrs. Roy Storey recalled a man carrying an empty bird cage and a little girl bearing the family strong box. The flood took out several bridges and innundated the lowlands. In dank, cramped conditions people waited days for the waters to subside enough for them to reoccupy the town. When they did finally return they had to shovel mud out of their homes.

By the next year the community had rebounded and was energetically laboring on the Commercial Waterway, as the Cedar River diversion was called. On June 1 a community picnic inaugurated the start-up of construction, and within months a new channel 80 feet long and 2,000 feet wide carried the river to the lake.

As this effort was nearing completion, work was well underway on the canal connecting the lake with the Sound. By the spring of 1916 the locks and dam at the Salmon Bay narrows were completed, as was the Fremont Cut connecting Salmon Bay with Lake Union. Work on the Montlake Cut connecting Lake Union with Lake Washington was in its final phase, and the stage was set for the lowering of the latter by eight feet. In July the spillway at the end of the Montlake Canal was opened, and the comingled waters of Lake Washington and the Cedar River tumbled into Lake Union. For four months the flow continued until by October the level of the two lakes had become equal.

With the 1911 organization of the Port of Seattle and the 1914 opening of the Panama Canal, optimism regarding industrial growth soared, but not all were pleased with the consequences. How could the Duwamish rejoice in the fact that the Black River, which had sustained them for centuries, was about to die? Moreover, the lowering of the lake would destroy sockeye salmon spawning grounds and would result in the withering of the wapato plant whose nutritious bulbs grew in the shallows. On the Black River, spawning salmon struggled fitfully in the shrunken stream. Joseph Moses, son of James Moses and a grandson of a Duwamish headman, recalled the last days of the river:

The Pacific Coast Coal factory at Renton was able to handle a capacity of 500 tons every eight hours. In this 1925 view, the Seattle PTA inspects the storage bins at the briquette factory on Houser Way. Courtesy, Renton Historical Society and Museum

That was quite a day for the white people at least. The waters just went down, down, until our landing and canoes stood dry and there was no Black River at all. There were pools, of course, and the struggling fish trapped in them. People came from miles around, laughing and hollering and stuffing the fish into gunny sacks.

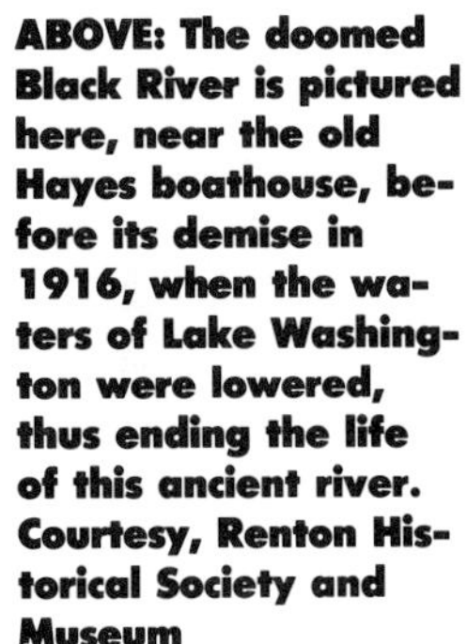

ABOVE: The doomed Black River is pictured here, near the old Hayes boathouse, before its demise in 1916, when the waters of Lake Washington were lowered, thus ending the life of this ancient river. Courtesy, Renton Historical Society and Museum

Perhaps some among the Duwamish recalled the legendary fish of Cedar Lake that would turn themselves into swans if they were abused. Surely with the construction of the dam on Cedar Lake, the diversion of the Cedar River, and the lingering death of the Black River, the spirits were being sorely tried.

It is left to us to make the mythic connection between that ecological disturbance and an event that occurred on June 15, 1916. On the east side of Lake Union a float plane built by William Boeing and Conrad Westervelt was launched from a hangar and powered up for its maiden flight, with Boeing as pilot. Taxiing over the water, its engines revved, the plane lifted gracefully into the air. From the water, wings had indeed risen.

As Boeing and Westervelt's plane made more test flights, wildlife continued to flee the river. But as in earlier transformations, this was not the end; it merely marked a change of worlds. One avenue for existence had disappeared, but the tide of life had now taken to the air, and Renton—native village; farming community; mining, commercial, and industrial center—entered upon a new era.

LEFT: The year of 1900 was a high watermark year for Renton, when melting snow caused all of the valley's rivers to rise and flood. Residents on the flat valley floor scrambled for higher ground, while high land neighbors helped with moving and opened up their homes until they overflowed with refugees. Courtesy, Renton Historical Society and Museum

CHAPTER 4

Building a Community

Renton supported many different types of athletics, including this rugby team. Courtesy, Renton Historical Society and Museum

A city is more than just buildings, streets, and sewers. It is first a community of people who live and work together and share, to varying degrees, a common identity. Building a community is no less a labor than nailing together a town; indeed, it requires greater devotion and skill, since human nature, while a durable compound, is less easily worked than wood, brick, or stone. The building of the Renton community was a long and painstaking process that began long before the town was platted or incorporated, and the early period of its growth was crucial to its later success.

In the 1880s the area bounded by Renton's present city limits encompassed a scattering of hamlets and homesteads. Eventually their population coalesced into a single community, but initially it was dispersed among a hodgepodge of

James (Jim) Moses moved with his father William from the Puget Sound area, where the Duwamish had been 'relocated,' back to Renton in 1856. His family felt that they should remain on their traditional land, even though the government was pressuring all Duwamish to move to reservations. Courtesy, Renton Historical Society and Museum

RIGHT: Jennie Moses raised her family on the acre of land deeded to her by Erasmus Smithers. Though her husband, James, died when their children were young, Jennie supported her family from the proceeds of her handicrafts and the kindness of neighbors and local businessmen. She is pictured here in 1921. Courtesy, Renton Historical Society and Museum

groups that had little in common and were sometimes at odds with one another.

A particularly onerous division was that separating native Americans from the settlers. It was not until the 1870s that settlers along the Black River outnumbered the native people who continued to live there, but the alien status of native people off the reservation and memories of the Yakima War colored relations between them. Twice, settlers petitioned to have the Duwamish removed to reservations, and on one occasion federal officials took a steamboat to William's Camp on Erasmus Smithers' land to order their removal. Chief William and his people were told to gather their belongings and board the steamer; after listening respectfully to the agent, William gave his reply. The gist of it was preserved by the Reverend George Whitworth:

> **William replied that the father in Olympia, or the Great Father in Washington City, had no right to remove his tribe. They were peaceful, had done no wrong. They were under no obligation to the government, had received nothing at its hands, and had asked for nothing. They had entered into no treaty; indeed, their lands had been taken from them. William had been born on Cedar River; there he intended to remain, and there his bones should be laid. He and his people were not willing to be removed. They could not be removed. Soldiers might be brought to take them away, but when the soldiers should come his people would not be found, for they would flee and hide themselves in the "stick" (the woods) where the soldiers could not search them out.**

A way out of the impasse was provided by Diana Smithers, who protested that those petitioning for the removal neither lived in the area nor knew the Duwamish. She and her husband, she went on, permitted them to stay on their land, and when he was away on business, she regarded their presence as protective. With a shrug the officials got back aboard the boat and steamed down the river. So the Duwamish could stay, although Joseph Moses recalled his father's persistent fear: "Yes, my dad stayed on, but I want to tell you something. Every day of his life he lived in fear that he'd see some white man coming down that path waving legal papers."

When Erasmus Smithers died in 1900, he deeded James' wife, Jennie, the land on which their house stood. There she raised her sons and kept alive some of the old traditions. A longtime resident, Frank Littlefield, recalled her with affection:

Though most of the local Chinese worked in the mines, some found other positions in the community, such as this young Chinese man (left), who was the cook for this early Renton boardinghouse. Courtesy, Renton Historical Society and Museum

My memories of Indians in Renton are tied in with the Moses family who were very kind and friendly people. Henry Moses became one of my best boyhood friends. His mother was a wonderful woman and visited my parents frequently, bringing Henry and his brother, Joe, with her. Many times she would bring fresh salmon or trout but the most important thing she brought was her kindness.

A few other native people eventually gained title to land. In 1897, Tenas Bill and his wife, Nellie, sold two acres on the shore of Lake Washington to Ferry Fay Burrows, who built a locally famous fishing resort on the property.

Another much abused group were the Chinese, who began entering western Washington in the 1870s to work on the railroads. They did most of the work on the S&WW line, directed by Chun Chin Hock, Seattle's best known labor contractor. The conflict with white workers that dogged the Chinese in the territory erupted locally in 1874, a recession year, when whites who wanted their jobs briefly drove them off the line.

In Renton most of the Chinese worked in the mines. The 1880 census enumerated 27 Chinese miners and farmers in the Renton area—all men in their twenties. An article "From the Fraser to the Columbia" in the May 1884 *Harper's Monthly* described their settlement, presumably the same quarters a *Pacific Tribune* writer located a half-mile below the Talbot Mine entrance:

Down at Renton the Chinese have built for themselves among the trees a group of small huts, steep-roofed, weather-reddened, and long-shingled; have planted narrow gardens on the river bank and have set up tiny coops for the beloved ducks and chickens, until they have made as picturesque and foreign a scene as though it were a home village on the Yang-tse-Kiang.

In all likelihood this community disappeared during the mid-1880s. In many areas of the West, white workers, fearful of losing their jobs, drove Chinese workers out of their communities. In 1885-1886, mobs of angry whites drove the Chinese from many western Washington settlements.

Black Americans also led a precarious existence in the area. The 1880 census noted only one black in Renton, 55-year-old Nelson Johnson, a farmer from Maryland. However, in 1891 the Oregon Improvement Company, which owned and operated the mines at Newcastle and Franklin, brought in several hundred

Black miners working at the Newcastle mine formed their own association, the Lime Kiln Club, in the late 1890s. Courtesy, Renton Historical Society and Museum

black miners, many with families, as strikebreakers, a fact few of them were aware of until they arrived. At a time when laws severely restricting black labor and residence were in force nationwide, blacks desperate for jobs were, like the Chinese, used often as pawns by company bosses in their battles against labor unions, most of which refused to admit blacks.

In spite of the antipathy directed against them, most of these new arrivals stayed, and in 1894 several black families in Newcastle signaled their intent to put down roots by organizing a Baptist church. Among ethnic groups on the frontier, churches served as important nuclei around which a sense of community developed, and this was especially true of blacks, for whom a church often represented the community's chief financial investment. At the turn of the century, several black families moved from Newcastle to what is now Kennydale and organized another church which survived until the 1940s.

The difficulties encountered by immigrant groups were largely caused by the region's unstable economy. Lumbering and mining followed a roller coaster boom and bust cycle. During booms jobs went begging and wages were high, but when booms went bust wages plummeted, jobs disappeared, and armies of unemployed tramped the country, looking for work. There were no social welfare programs to cushion the impact of unemployment, and when jobs were scarce competition for them heightened racial and ethnic animosities, retarding the development of a stable, tolerant society.

Haunting the region were other groups about whom only sketchy records survive. The Rom, better known as Gypsies, gathered annually in a camp by the Black River during the summer months. There were also Japanese who worked as section hands on the railroad, in lumber camps and mines, or as servants in homes. In time Japanese truck farmers carved out a valuable economic niche for themselves.

Foreign-born residents made up a third of all those counted by 1880 census takers in the Renton area. Of these, immigrants from the British Isles constituted the largest group, 78 in all, followed by the Chinese (27), Canadians (12), Germans (8), Danes (5), Norwegians (4), Belgians, Bohemians, French, and Italians (2 each), 1 Finn, and 1 Swede.

Francis Hayes and his wife, Sarah,

RIGHT: Both young and grizzled, the colorful faces of these Chinese, black, and white Coal Creek miners illustrate the diversity of ethnic backgrounds found in the Renton community in the 1880s. Notice their cap-mounted carbide lamps, which are still ablaze. Courtesy, Renton Historical Society and Museum

The tent houses of Coal Creek offered the bare minimum in housing for the mine's workers in 1917. Courtesy, Renton Historical Society and Museum

moved to Renton in 1880. Born in England in the 1830s, they married in Gloucestershire and emigrated to the United States, settling first in Philadelphia, then moving to Pittsburgh. In 1869 they traveled to Nortonville, California, where son John was born. In 1872 the family moved to Seahome (Bellingham), where Francis worked in the coal mines. Five years later the family moved to Newcastle.

The move from Seahome to Newcastle on the rough edge of the frontier remained a vivid memory for the Hayes family. It was spring when they made the 12-hour trip from Seahome on the sidewheeler *Libby* to Seattle, where they disembarked in a driving rain. A muddy two-mile hike through the woods brought them to Belltown, where an open coach took them on a jarring three-mile ride to Lake Washington. They arrived at the lake, dripping wet, and boarded another steamer that took them across to Murphy's Landing (Hazelwood). From there they trudged up the hill to Newcastle.

After they moved to Renton, 10-year-old John went to work with his father in the Talbot Mine as a "trapper," opening and closing tunnel doors built to control air circulation as mules passed by pulling coal cars. Sarah, however, believed a mine was no place for a boy, and he went to work instead greasing skids in logging camps. John, better known as Jack, grew up in Renton, attended its schools, worked on the railroad, played baseball on the local team, married, and raised a family. When he died in 1961 he had lived longer in Renton than any other resident.

In many respects the Hayes' story is typical of many other immigrants' experiences. After arriving in the United States they often moved several times, sometimes great distances, before settling in Renton, but once here they put down roots. For miners, especially, the penultimate stops on their journeys were neighboring coal towns such as Newcastle and Black Diamond.

The reasons for this pattern were the reasons why Renton flourished while other towns faded away. In the 1880s Newcastle's population was larger than Renton's, but it and towns such as Black Diamond and Franklin were company towns owned by the corporations operating the mines. Miners hoisted beers in company saloons while they and their families lived in company houses and traded at company stores. If a company wished to get rid of its workers, it could simply order them off the property. This happened at Black Diamond, and the action so infuriated Welsh homesteader Timothy Morgan that he offered lots on the land he owned nearby to the union and the displaced workers; the settlement that developed there was named Morgantown. A similarly organized settlement at Newcastle was called Unionville, and ultimately, companies found it in their interest to sell land to their workers.

Renton was never a company town. From the beginning, individuals were able to obtain title to land. The presence of privately owned stores and shops obviated the need for a company store, and competition between them kept prices at a reasonable level. Surrounded by company towns, Renton beckoned as a place where one could buy a house of one's own, to settle down and raise a family.

The appearance of a post office, first at Black Bridge in 1867 and then at Renton itself in 1876, as well as schools, marked the first stir-

The developing community of Renton relied on the goods and services of Thomas Harries' retail establishment, the Renton Cash Grocery. Harries (right) is shown here with his son Jack (left) and the store's delivery wagon in the early 1900s. Courtesy, Renton Historical Society and Museum

rings of community life. This life was nurtured by the activities of fraternal orders and benevolent societies. By 1877 the Renton Lodge, No. 61, of the International Order of Good Templars, a society dedicated to temperance work, was organized, and in August of that year it sponsored a picnic on William Smith's property, where Renton's brass band serenaded its members. Freemasons organized Saint Andrew's Lodge, No. 35, at Newcastle in 1879, but moved to Renton the following year. In 1884 the Independent Order of Odd Fellows (I.O.O.F.) instituted Renton Lodge, No. 28. In 1889 the women's Columbine Rebekah Lodge, No. 117, was chartered, and in 1899 the Nesika Chapter of the Order of the Eastern Star, another women's group, received its charter, taking its name Nesika, meaning "our," from the Chinook Jargon, a choice reflecting the friendly relations many members had with local native Americans. In 1907 Renton Aerie 1722 of the Fraternal Order of Eagles was organized.

With their hermetic traditions and celebratory rituals, these groups provided members with a sense of belonging often lacking on the frontier, where family ties were much weakened by distance. Meetings and picnics offered opportunities for socializing, and the organizations also provided members with health and funeral insurance. "No Eagle sleeps in the potters field" was one group's motto, and some Masonic organizations even retained physicians to serve their members.

Churches also worked to build community. The Presbyterian church had been there first, but two others—First Baptist, organized in 1901, and St. Anthony's Catholic Church, organized the same year as a mission—served as havens for several of Renton's ethnic groups.

First Baptist was the spiritual home to many of Renton's Welsh families. In September 1901, 18 Baptists met in the Odd Fellows Hall to organize the church. A heated discussion flared between Welsh members of the congregation who wanted the church's name changed to the Welsh Baptist Church and members who could not understand the Welsh language; the issue was settled with an agreement to organize a Welsh Sunday school. Money to build a church and hire a pastor was raised with innumerable teas and chicken dinners, and one of the first purchases for the new church was an organ to accompany the choir, so dear to the Welsh. In 1907 the church succeeded in acquiring the services of Robert Roberts, a Welsh immigrant noted for his skill as a choirmaster, who had actually paid for his and his wife's passage to America with prize monies won in choir competitions in Wales.

St. Anthony's parish came into being as priests from the surrounding area made visits to private homes to celebrate the Mass. The names of these homeowners—Thomas Nelligan, Dan Hogan, and John Sedlacek—recall the Irish and Slavic backgrounds of many early parishioners. Earlier, Duwamish Catholics such as the families of James Moses and Benjamin

Local benevolent societies and fraternal orders provided a variety of social activities and events for their members. The Nesika Chapter 54 of the Order of the Eastern Star pose for this portrait in 1903. Courtesy, Renton Historical Society and Museum

Many of Renton's immigrant families underwent harsh but sometimes enjoyable experiences in traveling to the area. Members of the Danielson family were photographed playing what seems to be a game of shuffleboard on the deck of a ship, while en route from Sweden to Renton in the early 1900s. Courtesy, Renton Historical Society and Museum

Solomon had attended services in a chapel Ben Solomon had built in his home on the Cedar River, near the community of Elliott. A bell called the faithful to morning and evening prayers, and on occasion a priest assigned to a nearby reservation would visit to say Mass and administer sacraments. After St. Anthony's was organized, many of these Duwamish Catholics became parishioners.

Another ethnic group whose names appear on the parish rolls were the Italians. Often those who worked in the mines would settle in Renton after living in nearby towns. Giacomo Gigli emigrated from Civago, Italy, in 1903. Arriving in New York, he traveled to San Francisco and thence to Jackson, Colorado, before coming to Black Diamond. In 1906 his wife, Fortunata, and their daughter, Celide, joined him there, and a year later the family moved to Renton, where he purchased a home from his cousin, Orestes Gaspari, another coal miner, who had come to Renton in 1901.

Many Italian men would work in the United States, save their money, marry in Italy, and eventually bring their wives over. Rinaldo Romiti, another arrival from Civago, came to Renton in 1906 and worked for the Denny-Renton Coal Company. Returning to Italy, he married Providenza Poli in 1909 and then came back to earn enough money to bring his wife and their young son, Adolph, to Renton in 1913.

Not all Italians worked in the mines. As others came, often on the advice of friends and relatives, they found jobs in other industries or opened businesses of their own. Locally there were Italian grocery stores, a dairy farm, a shoe repair shop, and even a macaroni factory, the Columbus Macaroni Factory, founded by Batista Agnesani and A. Gebenini in the early 1900s.

Many immigrants honored the memories of their homelands by maintaining ethnic and national customs. These were often centered in the home or church, as were the songfests held

Family gatherings and celebrations broke the monotony of daily work in Renton's early years. Here, the Varelli family gathers with friends to enjoy a holiday. Note the cask of wine and early phonograph. Courtesy, Renton Historical Society and Museum

by the Welsh to honor St. David's Day, the patron saint of Wales, on March 1. Scottish families celebrated the New Year with Hogmanay, when costumed children begged candy from passers-by and guests visited households at midnight. The first one to enter the door, the "first-footer," was expected to bring pastries or a bottle of spirits.

Among native Americans, a spirited revival of traditions occurred in 1894 when the Duwamish challenged kin and friends on the Puyallup Reservation to a "sing-gamble," a gambling match held in the house of Doctor Jack, a shaman, on the Cedar River three-quarters of a mile north of town. Sixteen wagons and several buggies brought Puyallup families to the gathering while others walked; several hundred people were welcomed by Chief William, Dr. Jack, and Jack Foster, another headman. For five days and nights participants feasted, socialized, and helped sing the mesmerizing chants that called forth the gamblers' powers. The contest seesawed between the Duwamish and the Puyallups, but in the end it was declared a draw, and everyone went away happy and invigorated.

Among the Duwamish, winter dances continued to be held, and Jack Hayes recalled attending them north of town with his girl. George Conklin, recently hired as principal of Central School, made friends with many native people and attended dances hosted by Doctor Bill, a Snoqualmie shaman, at the community of Indian on the Cedar River. In the winter of 1899-1900, one of the last spirit canoe ceremonies was held by the Duwamish on the Cedar River. The spirit boards and other paraphernalia used in this dramatic ritual were collected by professional ethnographers George Dorsey and Stewart Culin for the University Museum in Philadelphia.

Ethnic groups also introduced their own particular sports. Bocce ball, a popular Italian form of lawn bowling, was played during large picnics on meadows by the river or in well-tended courts. Finnish miners in Newcastle practiced gymnastics and held exhibitions in the Finnish Brotherhood Hall in the neighborhood known, inevitably, as "Finntown." Another practice Finns brought over with them from the old country was taking sauna baths, and several families built saunas next to their homes.

ABOVE: Dario Bulgarelli arrived from Italy in 1913, and began work at the Denny-Renton Clay and Coal plant in Taylor. When the Taylor operations closed, he then moved to Renton and worked at the company's Renton plant. Bulgarelli's heritage remained a proud part of his past, illustrated by his membership in the Sons of Italy. Courtesy, Renton Historical Society and Museum

Probably the most popular sport in Renton at the turn of the century was soccer, a favorite among immigrants hailing from the British Isles, especially. According to the late Renton historian Morda Slauson, a question commonly asked of one seeking a job at the mines was, "Will you play soccer?" Coal companies and local businesses sponsored teams and supplied uniforms, and on Sundays crowds gathered at Smithers' pasture or City Park to watch the local lads have at visiting teams. Renton teams played rival teams from as far afield as Portland and Nanaimo, a coal mining town on the British Columbia coast.

As the children of these soccer playing immigrants grew up and sought to distance themselves from the customs of their parents, many took an avid interest in the quintessential American game of baseball. At the turn of the century, baseball in Renton was about as American as it

LEFT: The Pozza family, pictured here in 1911, was one of the many Italian families who lived and worked in the Renton area. Courtesy, Renton Historical Society and Museum

BELOW: The spirited "sing-gamble" was a popular social event in Renton's native American community in the late 1800s. Courtesy, Renton Historical Society and Museum

OPPOSITE, TOP: Croquet proved to be a suitable sport for Newcastle residents, even when properly manicured lawns were unavailable. Courtesy, Renton Historical Society and Museum

OPPOSITE, BOTTOM: Central School initially housed grades one through eight, but later added high school classes. These young pupils of local teacher Mrs. Gunn rigidly pose for their class portrait in the early 1900s. Courtesy, Renton Historical Society and Museum

could get. The town's team was made up, with the exception of Jack Hayes, entirely of native Americans and named, appropriately enough, the Renton Indians. Eventually baseball became more popular than soccer, and by World War I it dominated the local sports scene.

In 1901 Renton was incorporated as a fourth-class town. Its charter gave its officers the right to collect taxes and submit bonds to voters to finance public works and pay the salaries of the mayor and town council members who were elected yearly. Renton now governed its own affairs.

Actually, it had already begun to do so in an interesting sort of way in 1895 when underemployed miners formed the Renton Cooperative Coal Company and reopened the mines which had been closed for nearly a decade. Miners were paid on a piecework basis, and each was restricted to loading only four cars a day. Critics contended that more energy was expended in company meetings than in digging coal, and production never exceeded 38,000 tons during any of the six years the Co-op operated the mines. By comparison, the Black Diamond mine produced 227,538 tons in 1899 alone. In 1901 the Co-op sold its holdings to the Seattle Electric Company, which greatly expanded production. Still, while it was in business, the Co-op provided jobs, and workers learned that they could be their own bosses.

If Renton was not a company town, neither was there much distance between workers and bosses. Early on there had been a nascent division of the town into a working-class district along the railroad tracks and a middle-class residential district on Earlington Hill.

The latter was set apart by the relatively palatial summer homes of luminaries such as historian Clarence Bagley, ex-territorial governor Elisha P. Ferry, and gentleman farmer William Smith in North Renton. The grounds of their estates served as parks where Seattleites came for rustic picnics, but once sold by their owners, these estates were put to different uses. The Bagley mansion served briefly as headquarters of *Western Magazine,* a popular but short-lived publication, and then as the clubhouse for what became the Earlington Country Club, site of one of the state's first golf courses. The Smith house, abandoned around the turn of the century, gained a reputation among local children as a haunted house.

As estates were broken up into lots and sold, new houses were built on them. Homes also marched up Renton Hill as the Co-op sold lots from its holdings, and the middle-class and working-class came to live side by side in the best Northwestern tradition.

As more people moved to Washington,

townspeople worked to make Renton an attractive place to live. Of great concern was improvement of the quality of local schools. David Parker recalled that while the county school superintendent, Edmund Carr, lived in Renton, he and many others sent their children to schools in Seattle. High school classes were offered for the first time in 1902 when George Conklin began teaching 9th and 10th grades, and in 1904 the first graduates received their diplomas. One challenge Conklin had to face was the lack of discipline among the older boys. Bullies had driven out two principals before he arrived; he solved the problem with his fists in the first days of his tenure.

Another shortcoming was the lack of an adequate library. Initially the school library had consisted of a shelf of books in the principal's office in Central School; these were supplemented by books from a town lending library organized in 1903 by retired Welsh miner Evan Davis of the Renton Miners Association. The pressing need for a larger public library prompted Neva Bostwick, a prominent Earlington Hill resident, to obtain a grant from the Carnegie Library Foundation for the construction in 1914 of Renton's first public library, on land donated by Ignazio Sartori.

By then Renton also had its first hospital, a two-story frame building with 15 rooms and an operating area, built by Dr. Adolph Bronson, a physician practicing in Renton since

Sparkling starched dresses and elaborate hair ribbons adorn the participants of the 1911 May Pole dance. Courtesy, Renton Historical Society and Museum

Baseball was one of Renton's most popular sports, at the school, professional, and recreational levels. Townspeople vigorously supported the teams of their choice, and welcomed a sizzling baseball game on a warm Sunday afternoon. Courtesy, Renton Historical Society and Museum

1905. In it residents injured through mine and mill accidents could receive care close to home, and in time many of the community's children were born there.

Some of the most vivid recollections of Renton's early days are those preserved in childhood memories. Before movies came to town, many young people entertained themselves peering through the windows of the Melrose Saloon and marveling at the trough beneath the bar that ran water to extinguish cigar butts. More memorable were the times when the owner hired a man to put on shows with his performing bear.

Even though it was an industrial town, rivers, lakes, and farmlands bordered Renton, and nature was never far away. Dail Butler Laughery recalled that while her childhood in North Renton was made busy by chores, such as cleaning lamp chimneys with newspaper and drawing water from a well to fill pitchers for each bedroom, there was still time to roam fields knee-high with buttercups and gather them by the armful or to pick buckets of delicious wild berries. As the town grew, however, this rural setting retreated, and Laughery remembered being distraught when the huge maple trees that fronted her family's property and supported swings fell before the tide of municipal expansion:

Progress was coming to North Renton and about 1909 our big maple trees were cut down to make way for a wooden sidewalk, and how I cried. To this day I never like to see a tree cut down unless it is absolutely necessary, and I just knew then that no sidewalk was as important as our swings in those big maple trees, where we could swing to the song of the meadow larks, and almost touch the sky with our toes.

Other memorable features of town life before the days of home appliances and convenience stores were the tradesmen who visited homes, such as the tool sharpener who put new edges on scissors, knives, and scythes, and the tinker who mended cooking ware. Inevitably, children followed his cart, singing, "Tom, Tom, the tinkerman, he mends your pans as quick as he can." Coal, ice, dairy products, and groceries were delivered house to house, as were fresh seasonal vegetables by a man in a cart, who announced his arrival with the call, "Radishee!"

Birthdays, holidays, and deaths all brought families and friends together to mark the passing of life's important events. The Telban and Blazich families gather to celebrate the christening of a new Blazich family member, circa 1915. Courtesy, Renton Historical Society and Museum

Almost everyone turned out to celebrate festivals like May Day, when school children dressed as flowers and rain drops sang songs, wound ribbons around a maypole, and helped crown the Queen of the May. The high point of summer was the Fourth of July, a day-long extravaganza during which native-born and immigrant alike celebrated the nation's birth. It began usually at 10 P.M. with a parade, billed on one program as the "Calithumpian." Crowds cheered from sidewalks as the brass band marched by and volunteer firemen proudly drove their shiny new pumper down the street, followed by wagonloads of children, each waving a flag. At City Park firemen gave the children ice cream, and townswomen provided a huge picnic lunch replete with Old World delicacies. There were games and athletic contests: canoe and boat races, a greased-pig chase, a tug-of-war, and in the afternoon, a baseball game. In the velvet air of evening, couples danced to waltzes played by the band in the park pavilion.

At the opposite pole of the year, the community put up a Christmas tree in a building or hall and decorated it with popcorn strings, paper chains, and children's gifts hung from its boughs. On Christmas Eve choirs sang; trays of cookies and pastries were served, and each child received a paper cone filled with nuts, candy, and perhaps an orange. Gradually this community celebration moved into the churches, each of which displayed its own tree. Parents sometimes brought presents to church and gave them to their children there.

As community life grew more complex and interdependent and the town developed a history of its own, the significance of events in its life broadened. People measured the progress of their lives by recalling notable floods, fires, the construction of new buildings, or holdups on the Interurban. All shared the grief of mine disasters: the explosion at Coal Creek in 1894 that killed 4 men, a fire and explosion at Franklin that same year that killed 37, an explosion at Black Diamond in 1902 that killed 12, and another at Ravensdale in 1915 that killed 31. Nothing so destructive occurred in Renton itself, but many in town were related to the victims and their families.

On the lighter side, there was the time when the notorious Western outlaw Harry Tracy, a member of Butch Cassidy's "Hole in the Wall" gang, passed through Renton after escaping from the Oregon State Penitentiary in Salem in 1902. He spent an easy afternoon chatting with three women in the Jarrell house near Elliott until he heard footsteps outside.

Community spirit continued to thrive in Renton, resulting in some unique attempts to draw attention to the town. Especially notable was the use of a promotional rocket, which was launched from the top of Mount Rainier on Labor Day in 1916. Courtesy, Renton Historical Society and Museum

These were Jack Duncalf's, a Renton butcher who, Winchester rifle in hand, was anxious to win the $6,000 bounty on Tracy's head. Seeing Duncalf skulking about outside, Tracy inquired who he was, but did not quite believe the story told him that he was simply a Renton butcher out looking for stray cattle. Bidding the ladies adieu, Tracy made his escape, eluding Duncalf as well as the county sheriff, who came puffing up the road with a pack of bawling bloodhounds. He would meet a violent end a few weeks later in an eastern Washington wheat field.

They were innocent days in 1916 when the Renton Commercial Club hired Major E.S. Ingraham, one of the first to climb Mount Rainier, to recruit climbers for a trek to its summit, where the party could set off fireworks to advertise a fair the town was holding on Labor Day. After wearing out three of the four cars on the trip to the mountain, the team reached the summit after a two-day climb. One of the party, John Lehman of Seattle, lit the rockets, and the glow of their bursts was seen by many in the low country. Another climber, Allen Hitching, recalled the experience: "We saw a big glow hanging over Seattle, another over Tacoma and two smaller glows over Kent and Auburn. John broke open the flare package and struck a match. The fourth one caught and the flares burned for about 10 minutes, making the sky as bright as day."

Seven months later, the United States entered World War I. The war caused profound changes throughout the nation, and like other cities in Washington, Renton would be powerfully affected. The year 1916 marked the end of an era, one that for all its troubles and hardships was full of optimism and enthusiasm. In a half-century Renton had grown from a few homesteads along the Black River to a thriving industrial center. Its people had weathered boom and bust, fire and flood, and had created a resilient community. The tribute given by an anonymous historical writer to Renton's immigrant groups could be applied as well to the whole community which had achieved so much:

This they had in common—they were God-fearing, law abiding, hard working citizens who believed in doing a day's work for a day's pay—they asked for no handouts. When times were hard they did the best they could with what they had. They established churches. They supported schools. They created parks. In short, they did all they could to see that their children and their children's children would have a better education—a better job—better living conditions—a better life and a better town than they had had. To them we owe a debt of thanks.

Idyllic and at peace, the Beil family and friends enjoy an afternoon of exchanging stories and listening to music. The serenity was soon interrupted, as America joined World War I and young men went off to war. Courtesy, Renton Historical Society and Museum

CHAPTER 5

An Interlude of Change

A joyous armistice celebration spanned many months in Renton as people rejoiced at the end of World War I. The following Fourth of July parade used the armistice theme to remind citizens of the current cherished peace. Courtesy, Renton Historical Society and Museum

The period between the beginning of World War I and the end of World War II was marked by profound and often unsettling change in Renton, as it was elsewhere. Population figures indicate the scope of this change. Renton had grown from 406 in 1890 to 1,176 in 1900, and by World War I the number approximated 3,000. Thereafter growth slowed; by 1940 the population had increased to only about 4,500, but in the next few years it soared as a flood of war industry workers poured in. By the end of World War II, Renton had more than 16,000 people.

The town's seven-fold population increase from 1890 to World War I reflected the growth of the region as it filled with people. In 1890 Washington State counted 357,232 people; by the war it had well over one million. The town

Hazardous and grim working conditions for impossibly low wages led workers at the Black Diamond Mine to organize a strong labor movement in the Northwest, which resulted in the formation of a local miners' union. Courtesy, Renton Historical Society and Museum

also benefited from Seattle's phenomenal growth in those years, nourished in part by the Yukon and Alaskan gold rushes.

Most who tried their luck in the northern gold fields met with indifferent success. After emigrating to the United States with his wife, Jane, Welshman Thomas Harries left the grimy diggings in Newcastle to seek his fortune in the Klondike. But after two unimpressive years there he returned, moved his family to Renton, and opened the Renton Cash Grocery, a more prosaic route to prosperity, but a dependable one. Four of pioneer Robert Wood's sons did better, each starting a business from money made in Alaska. Another man, Ben Atkinson, made enough to build the three-story Melrose Hotel on Wells South and Houser Way.

By 1917, Renton had become the commercial hub of the area south and east of Lake Washington. Coal contributed to its prosperity, but by then, mining employed fewer people than did the town's other industries. Indeed, save for a brief resurgence during the war, the local coal industry had entered upon a decline from which it would never recover.

The coal of Renton and Newcastle was low grade, and the high cost of extracting it meant that companies operated on thin profit margins even in flush times. These margins shrank even more when the completion of transcontinental railroads made superior coal from the Rocky Mountain states widely available at low prices. But the death of the local coal industry came with the introduction of new energy sources: California petroleum and hydroelectricity.

Symptomatic of the industry's decline was an increase in conflict between labor and management. In 1907 the United Mine Workers Union began organizing miners in Black Diamond, and in June 1912 miners in Renton organized and went on strike, demanding that their employer, the Puget Sound Traction, Light and Power Company, recognize the union and negotiate with it.

The company responded by firing the strikers and hiring strikebreakers, and in January 1914 it succeeded in forcing the workers to return. The union had failed, but the situation improved with the war, when the government rationed oil and the demands of war industries sent coal production in the state to its historic high: 4,128,124 tons in 1918. Employment in the mines was so high that there was a housing shortage in Newcastle, and in Renton, Pacific Car and Foundry was operating full blast to meet a government order for 1,000 railroad cars.

RIGHT: When labor strikes hit the Renton coal mines, support came from the nationally organized unions and from the miners' families. In 1911, the women's local gathered to make their point with a sign which read, "United We Stand/ United We Fall/We Stand For Our Riches/Or Nothing AT ALL." Courtesy, Renton Historical Society and Museum

Renton waxed patriotic as its young men enlisted. There were war bond drives; women wrapped bandages, and knitted socks for the soldiers passing by in troop trains; and City Park's name was changed to Liberty Park.

But the war also excited antipathies among certain immigrant groups. Italians and Austrians paid close attention to news of action on the Italian front, and the success of the Austrian armies after the battle of Caporetto in October 1917 inspired taunting shouts of "No more macaroni!" in the mines.

The economy suffered a sharp decline after the Armistice was signed in 1919. Coal production plummeted, and a glut of railroad cars brought the car shops to a standstill, except for work being done on a new line of logging trucks. After an output of 58 million bricks in 1917 that made the Denny-Renton Clay and Coal Company the world's largest producer of paving brick, its employees also felt the pinch of the downturn. Their problems were compounded by a dwindling market for paving brick as automobile use changed the way roads were built.

In response to these changes, workers were let go and wages were slashed. Despite the failure of the 1919 Seattle general strike, the United Mine Workers refused a request from operators to cut wages, and in March 1921 local mines shut down and workers were locked out. When it was learned that strikebreakers were being brought in from Montana, picket lines appeared. Whole families took part, roasting potatoes near the rail depot as they waited for trains carrying the strikebreakers to arrive.

Tensions mounted. After a pastor made a sympathy visit to a strikebreaker's home, union members in his congregation succeeded in forcing his removal. Some strikers even climbed Renton Hill above the mine opening and fired shotguns at the strikebreakers as they came out of the mine for lunch.

After miners in Newcastle and other company towns were evicted from their houses, Renton gained in population. In 1923 the strike collapsed, and the remaining workers returned to the mines at lower wages. The sad affair hastened the end of the local coal industry and the coal towns themselves, save Renton, which survived to prosper.

The postwar period was difficult socially as well as economically. Even before the war fear had been widespread that the massive influx of immigrants from southern and eastern Europe threatened to "pollute" American culture. Pseudo-scientists sought to demonstrate the inferiority of Slavs and Italians by measuring their skulls, and demagogues called for curbs on immigration and the expulsion of undesirables. Responding to this antipathy, many ethnic groups organized protective associations as they did in Renton in 1919, a year of labor unrest, when the Slovenian National Brotherhood and the Star of Italy Lodge were formed.

Many farmers, who earlier had organized several local granges for purposes of mutual

The call to serve in World War I reached across the continent to Renton. Art Beil's army troop from Renton trained in San Antonio, Texas, and later served in battle overseas. Beil's troop is shown here circa 1917, while training at Fort Houston. Courtesy, Renton Historical Society and Museum

Between 1920 and 1930 changes continued to take place in Renton as it slowly evolved from a fledgling town to an urban center. Along Wells Street, asphalt replaced brick paving, businesses updated their signs or faded into history, and increased traffic required the installation of a traffic light. Courtesy, Renton Historical Society and Museum

aid, directed their economic anxiety toward immigrant Japanese, Filipino, and Mexican laborers, who allegedly spent their earnings outside the area, and toward Japanese farmers who owned or leased land and whose competition they feared. Under pressure from farmers, the Washington State legislature passed an alien land law in 1921, banning Japanese immigrants from owning land. In Renton, Ijyuro Ishikawa, who had purchased land in 1912, and Gensaku Shiubara, who leased 40 acres for his milk business, were threatened with the confiscation of their holdings, but each won his case in court.

At this time the Ku Klux Klan was active nationwide, fomenting religious, racial, and ethnic bigotry. The first state convention of the Klan in Washington State was held at Peoples Park at Renton Junction in July 1923. A large number of farmers and their families attended the day-long event and the evening fireworks display at Wilson Station, an interurban stop east of Orillia. Although some from Renton attended the convention, most residents were indifferent to it, and others had no tolerance for the Klan or other hate groups. Carrying out state law, King County Sheriff Matt Starwich prevented Klansmen from wearing their hoods, and when he discovered that one of his own deputies was a Klansman, he fired him.

Renton was changing. One had only to look out one's window to see that automobiles were replacing streetcars, that asphalt and concrete were replacing paving brick, or, block by block, that the wooden sidewalks for the frontier town were being replaced by concrete walks. As work crews tore up the planks, eager boys followed behind, looking for coins that had fallen through the cracks. Brick buildings replaced wooden ones, and overhead, poles carried an increasing tangle of telephone and electrical wires. In the 1920s Puget Power began offering free cooking classes taught by home economists to help women learn to use new electric ranges. Refrigerators and washing machines also made housework easier, and in the evenings families gathered around that new wonder, the radio, for entertainment and news.

A good portion of news then described the efforts of lawmen who strove to halt or who sometimes participated in the illegal liquor trade. Virtually every year since incorporation, law and order in Renton had been kept by marshal Jack Stewart and after that by his son Vince, but other than their having to collar an occasional drunk or break up a fight now and then, Renton was a peaceable, law-abiding town. This began to change, however, in 1916 when enactment of a statewide prohibition law criminalized the production and sale of liquor. Many in town cherished traditions of wine and beer making, and the prices home brew fetched during prohibition tempted many to market their bootleg products.

The Stewarts had their hands full hunting down illegal stills in their jurisdiction, hidden often in cellars and mine shafts, but they were assisted by Sheriff Matt Starwich, whose diminutive frame belied his zeal and energy. Periodically, newspapers detailed raids in and around Renton, such as the discovery of a 107-gallon moonshine cache hidden in the brush along the Newcastle-Newport Road in 1924, or when Starwich discovered the largest still in King County, a 300-gallon monster, bubbling happily away in an abandoned house in Newcastle.

If there was evidence of widespread social discontent in the 1920s, there were also signs of social progress, for example, in the lives of women in the community. On the frontier, women enjoyed more opportunities than they did elsewhere in the country, and in Washington they even had the vote for a brief period in the 1880s, but they were not yet full partners in society. In 1891 Susan Harries Custer served Renton as postmistress for a year, but it was not until the vote was returned to them in 1910 that women were able to participate significantly in the community's political life. In 1919 Hattie Butler, Dail Butler Laughery's grandmother, ran for the position of councilman in the town's

LEFT: Though often considered to be less than full members of society, a number of women made meaningful contributions to the community. Susan Harries Custer served one year as the postmistress of Renton, succeeding her husband, Charles, after his death in 1890. Courtesy, Renton Historical Society and Museum

Civic-minded Agnes Edwards (second from left) held the position of Renton City Clerk for 19 years, one of the first women to hold a long-term position with the city. The other three city officers in this 1942 photograph are, from left to right: George Beanblossem, Agnes Dency, and Paul Houser, Sr. Courtesy, Renton Historical Society and Museum

The U.S. Junk Company opened in 1927 with a variety of new, used, and sometimes unusable merchandise. Several moves and a few name changes later, McLendon Hardware today continues to provide the largest assortment of hardware in the Northwest. Courtesy, Renton Historical Society and Museum

first ward and won. Learning of her victory after returning home from a shopping trip to Seattle, she observed wryly, "Here I leave home this morning a perfectly respectable housewife only to learn when I get home that I have been elected a councilman." Soon, other women assumed positions of responsibility. In 1923 Agnes Edwards became the first women to serve as city treasurer and clerk, and a year later Agnes Nordby Richardson, a recent law school graduate, served as city attorney.

But the progress everyone anticipated on the economic front came only grudgingly. Under new management Pacific Car and Foundry struggled to stay afloat financially. With still little market in railroad cars, it began fabricating bridge spans from structural steel. The Denny-Renton Clay and Coal Company limped along, supplying products for local construction, but in 1927 the Gladding McBean Company of California purchased the plant and began a long-overdue modernization, sparking hopes for its future. The Renton Sunbeam Coal Company and the Strain Coal Company still worked the mines, but production fell far short of what it had been in earlier years. The briquette factory still made briquettes out of coal dust, lumber and shingle mills continued to saw wood, and a number of "gyppo" outfits logged the forest cover ever longer distances from town.

Individually the industries were struggling, but together they provided a middling livelihood for Renton's citizens, whose trade managed to sustain First National Bank, the largest in King County outside Seattle. Commerce grew with population; many businesses began and remain as family-run enterprises. Back from the war and enamored neither of lumbering nor mining, Tom Rubattino and a friend purchased a hamburger stand in 1920 on Third Avenue and turned it into a Renton favorite, the Owl Cafe, ancestor of today's Rubattino's Restaurant. That same year Edward Stokes opened a mortuary that still bears his name. Most unique, however, was the "U.S. Junk Co. Store" opened in 1927 by Moses "Pop" McLendon, which evolved into McLendon Hardware, the largest independently owned hardware store in the Northwest.

New types of businesses appeared. With the advent of motion pictures, several movie theaters opened and quickly became places where one went to be seen as well as to see pictures flickering on the screen to the tremulous music of a pipe organ. The increasing popularity of automobiles inspired Max and Richard Clarke to open their Ford dealership in 1921, the same year Walt Reid and Henry and Walt Cook opened a filling station on the corner of Third and Burnett.

Automobile traffic in Renton increased with the development of the Sunset Highway, which left Seattle and passed around the southern end of the lake on its way to Snoqualmie Pass. By the middle 1920s, the road was paved as far as Bryn Mawr, and as traffic across the pass grew, auto camps—the forerunners of motels—sprang up at Renton and other towns along the route.

As auto travel increased, rail passenger service decreased. One victim of this trend was the Puget Sound Electric Railway—the Interurban—so beloved by Renton commuters. In 1919 the line carried more than three million passengers, along with fresh produce from valley farms, dairy products, and the mail. But trucks captured the mail route, and by 1927, with cars and buses carrying people and goods between towns along its route, the line went bankrupt. On December 31, 1928, the last train, filled with sentimental riders, made its final run from Seattle to Tacoma.

By then, passenger trains to Newcastle had also stopped running, although this was due less to competition from automobiles than to the gradual demise of the town. The same was true for local rail service up the Cedar

LEFT: The 1921 opening of a Ford dealership, owned by Richard and Max Clarke, introduced another aspect of transportation to Renton. At their second location on Bronson Way, the Clarke brothers display their tow truck, which was not exactly auspicious advertising for their new automobiles. Courtesy, Renton Historical Society and Museum

BELOW: One result of increasing automobile use in the Renton area was the construction of cabins to shelter passing campers. Leo Rosa's cabins at Main and Grady, pictured here in 1938, provided refuge not only for weary travelers, but for their vehicles as well. Courtesy, Renton Historical Society and Museum

River, which ended in 1925. The Seattle and Rainier Valley Railway, the successor to the old S&RB, began to lose customers to the Seattle Renton Stage Line that ran small buses called "Bluebirds" on the road paralleling the tracks. Unable to compete, the railroad lasted barely 10 years more.

Another sign of economic change took wing north of town on the new land created when the level of the lake was lowered. Early in 1922 a young man working for the Standard Oil plant in Renton, Frank Conklin, was making a delivery when he noticed work going on along the lake shore north of Bonnell's Nursery. A steel-wheeled tractor was scraping out a road to the shore, and on closer inspection Conklin discovered pilot Eddie Hubbard laying planks on the sand for a seaplane landing.

Hubbard had worked as a test pilot for William Boeing during and after the war, and in 1920 he won a contract from the U.S. Postal Service to deliver mail by air in Boeing aircraft from Seattle to Victoria. By the summer of 1922, he had a 2,300-foot, north-south, dirt-and-sand runway built on the flats below Bryn Mawr, and to the sound of the coal hoist whistle, the whine of sawmills, and the clangor of the car shops was added the drone of aircraft as Hubbard flew his appointed rounds on gas sold him by Conklin.

Later, in 1929, John Blum and his brother, Al, co-owners of Northwest Air Services, expanded their operations from Boeing Field on the Duwamish River to the runway at Bryn Mawr. In partnership with mine owner William Strain, the field was improved and several hangars were built near its lake end. Their company provided a flying school and a place where planes could be serviced, and pilots returning from Alaska during the winter came to the field to have their pontoons replaced with wheeled landing gear.

By the end of the 1920s, Renton looked a lot different than it had at the decade's beginning. In 1923 there was a new city hall, a two-story brick structure housing police and fire departments. A year later the organization of the Renton Savings and Loan Corporation marked the beginning of a modest boom in home construction, and in 1924 a plant supplying Pacific Car and Foundry with gas for cutting torches was built. The products of Gladding McBean and output from the town's new cement plant went into improvements in street, water, and sewage systems, as well as a new I.O.O.F. hall, an ice and ice cream plant, the remodeling of the Grand Theater, and new buildings like the Mikkelson Building, the Delaurenti Building, and the Edwards and Boas Building. To satisfy the local demand for electricity, Puget Power built the Shuffleton Steam Plant on the lakeshore, and when its first generator went on line in 1929, powered by Renton coal, it illuminated Renton's first street lights.

By any measure, Renton had become a more civilized place. It even enjoyed a certain amount of political discord, always a mark of urban sophistication. Pieter Prins, editor of the *Renton Stimulator,* a

Motion picture shows at Grand Theater could really draw a crowd, as this 1929 photograph illustrates. It is believed that this picture was taken the first night a movie with sound was shown in Renton. Courtesy, Renton Historical Society and Museum

biweekly paper published by the Service Station and Auto Park Association, took aim at the Renton Commercial Club in his columns. He hoped to organize a Kiwanis Club in opposition to the Commercial Club, but when it did organize in 1919 under the leadership of Richard Clarke, the organization devoted its energies instead to fund raising for youth projects.

Another group seeking to improve the community was the Earlington Women's Club, also organized in 1919. It pressed for more sidewalks and better lighting and collected for the Children's Orthopedic Hospital fund. It also sought to beautify their neighborhood by distributing packets of flower seeds to schoolchildren.

But the hopes residents nurtured for their area were put on hold as the shadow of the Great Depression spread across the land. As construction dropped off, there was little market for bricks or cement or lumber, and with fewer trees cut, there was little demand for rail cars or logging trucks to haul them. In 1928 Pacific Car and Foundry was busy building 1,000 cars; by 1931, the entire corporation to which it belonged, American Car and Foundry, had orders for only 35. In Renton there were layoffs and wage cuts, and some manufacturers simply disappeared.

Things limped along. People still had to keep warm, and coal production, although halved in 1930 by the closure of the Sunbeam mine, rebounded to near 1929 levels in 1931. The automobile had become so much a part of life that Hayden Williams and John Swanson opened a Chevrolet agency in 1931—and kept it open for more than 40 years. In 1931 construction of the main part of Renton High School, which replaced the older 1911 building, provided desperately needed jobs. Even Northwest Air Services survived until Seattle City Light's transmission lines across the Commercial Waterway made takeoffs and landings too dangerous.

In a pinch, people could still fish the Cedar River, collect firewood, go hunting, or plant a garden. Gyppo mining outfits sprang up as small groups of unemployed miners worked seams that were ignored in better times. At the end of 1931 the *Renton Chronicle* tried to put a brave face on things, writing: "There have been losses to take, it is true, and profitless balance sheets. But in the main our guns are still booming away and our flag still flies."

Garden clubs became a popular pastime in Renton, especially as efforts to beautify the city gained momentum. The first garden show took place in 1929 in front of the Ford dealership. Courtesy, Renton Historical Society and Museum

Three months later, however, the unemployed demonstrated in Renton's streets, demanding 45 cents an hour rather than the 33⅓ cents the county welfare board offered for work. Every penny counted, and this time the strikers held out until they won.

As the federal and state New Deal programs got organized, things gradually got better. In Washington State the 1933 repeal of prohibition was accompanied by a lifting of the ban on horse racing, and two racing enthusiasts, Joe Gottstein and William Edris, looked about for a suitable site to build a race track. The fine alluvium at Renton Junction looked promising, and after purchasing 107 acres of James Nelson's dairy farm, the two men put famed theater architect Marcus Priteca to work designing the racing complex. In 28 days the racing oval, grandstand, and jockeys' quarters were completed, and Longacres Racetrack opened for business on August 3. In drab times it was a brilliant success.

Good fortune also smiled on Pacific Car and Foundry in the person of metallurgist Alex Finlayson, who invented Carcometal, a strong, light steel alloy whose use in hoists and other items boosted sales. More good news came with the repurchase of the company by its original owner, William Pigott, whose energy and business acumen succeeded in putting the firm back on its economic feet. In 1934 Pigott was able to double the Renton plant's employment to 250.

Another bright spot was the Pacific

ABOVE: Spectators at the Longacres Racetrack jam the walkways and clubhouse during the 1933 season. Courtesy, Renton Historical Society and Museum

BELOW: Judging the winners at the Racetrack took a keen eye and an advantageous viewing location. Courtesy, Renton Historical Society and Museum

Coast Coal Company's opening of the New Black Diamond Mine near the community of Indian that same year. In its first year of operation, a work force of more than 300 produced 152,889 tons of coal, making it the most successful mine in local history. Production peaked in 1937 at 175,340 tons, the last burst of vigor in the local coal industry, and it could not have occurred at a better time. To commemorate the role coal miners played building the community, the Works Progress Administration commissioned artist Jacob Elshin in 1938 to paint the heroic murals that were hung in the lobby of the Renton Post Office.

These times were marked by the passing of two memorable figures whose lives had touched the people of Renton in two very different ways, one of international repute, the other, purely local, but hardly less significant. When Will Rogers and Wiley Post landed at the Bryn Mawr airfield in August 1935 to have their landing wheels replaced with pontoons for a trip to Alaska, it was the greatest aeronautical event in Renton since Charles Lindbergh flew over the town in 1928. A crowd gathered to see the famous Oklahoma humorist and actor, and when shy young Claude Hisey's mother coaxed him to ask the celebrity if he could take his picture, Rogers responded with an easy, "Sure, come ahead." It was one of the last photographs taken of him. After two days spent fishing in Elliott Bay and playing polo at Lake City, the two men flew on to Alaska where, a week later, they were killed when their plane crashed. The tragedy stunned the nation and left millions of Rogers' admirers grieving.

Grief also attended the burial of Jennie Moses in February 1937. Her father had come from a noble family on White River, and her mother from one on the Black, where she and James Moses had raised their family.

The funerals of well-regarded native figures had always brought whites and natives together. Before Chief William died in 1896, he asked his friend, Erasmus Smithers, to see that he was buried respectably and not like a "seedy old vagrant" as many newcomers regarded him. Smithers honored his request and saw to it that a fine headstone marked his grave at the Mount Olivet Cemetery. When James Moses died Fred Smithers paid for his funeral, and Tom Harries collected 79 silver dollars from friends, dropping them one by one into Jennie's apron during a sympathy visit. Sobbing with gratitude, she asked Smithers to be one of her husband's pallbearers, and he was the last to shake James' hand as he lay in his casket. Later, hundreds of family members and friends would gather at St. Anthony's Church to attend Jennie's Requiem Mass and to follow the hearse up to Mount Olivet, where she was laid to rest beside her husband.

In spite of hard times the community remained resilient and vigorous. Growth in the number of working women and those owning businesses led to the formation in 1934 of the Renton Business & Professional Women's Service Club, which soon counted nearly all working women among its membership. The community also continued in its devotion to the well-being of its children. As one of their fund-raising efforts for youth, Kiwanians began sponsoring citywide Halloween parties in 1930. In 1939 the first Renton Rodeo sponsored by the new Lions Club turned out to be such a success that members contributed $2,500 of their own money toward the second, which was an even greater success. Some 6,000 people attended, and the event attracted contestants from as far away as Montana.

Its wheels replaced with pontoons, Will Rogers and Wiley Post check their plane prior to their departure for Alaska in August 1935. A week later, Renton and the rest of America was shocked by the news that the two had died in a plane crash. Courtesy, Renton Historical Society and Museum

Early in 1940 the work of organizing Renton's first Lutheran Church was begun by the Reverend Sven J. Ristesund, a native of Norway. People of Scandinavian and German background had long been present in Renton, and individuals such as Strawberry Johnson, a Swede who owned a large strawberry patch near town, had become part of the local folklore, but those of Lutheran background were slow to develop a church until large numbers of people began to enter the area on the eve of war.

Even before the outbreak of World War II, the Northwest's economy had begun a notable expansion as the federal government poured money into huge projects like the Grand Coulee Dam. Pacific Car and Foundry's Structural Steel Divison built parts for this and other dams as well as for the Lake Washington Floating Bridge which opened in 1940. In 1941 the company was hard at work building railroad cars, another sign of the upturn, and it helped fabricate wings for the B-17 bomber Boeing was building for the U.S. Army Air Corps. After war had broken out in Europe, Boeing began building the bombers for Great Britain in its huge Plant Two beside the Duwamish River.

The company also had a contract with the navy to build a long-range flying boat, but since room was lacking at its Seattle facilities, it looked elsewhere. The south shore of Lake Washington beckoned, and early in 1941 work began to prepare the area for its new purpose. Slag from the Renton mine filled in swampy parts of the flats, and soon, immense new buildings rose on the graded surface.

Many felt war was imminent, but news of the December 7 attack on Pearl Harbor came as a shock and helped to precipitate a tragedy. Restricted by law from owning land, even from becoming citizens, Japanese-Americans were viewed by many with suspicion because they did not mix, and once the war began, the government drew up plans to remove them from the West Coast. There were not as many in Renton as in the Green River valley, but these were rounded up with the others in May 1942 and sent to a relocation camp at Puyallup. A retired teacher at the Henry Ford School recalled watching from her house that sad day as the evacuees were assembled at the freight siding on Burnett Avenue for the trip to Puyallup. Some had been her students in school; most lost their homes and businesses, and only a few ever returned.

The sense of the tragedy, however, was overwhelmed by the press of events. Industries on a war footing operated around the clock. Boeing's plans to build the flying boat were shelved—only one was built—and work commenced instead on the new B-29 high-altitude bomber. The first took wing at Renton in September 1942, and the plant was soon turning out 85 a month. At the same time, federal investment in a huge, new foundry enabled Pacific Car and Foundry to build an average of 30 Sherman tanks a month.

Where before jobs had been scarce, now labor was at a premium, and local businesses found it difficult to keep their employees. Tom Rubattino recalled the problems he had running his restaurant:

I had some real good men cooks but just when we were busiest, they'd turn up missing or drunk. I don't know what I would have done without my wife, Helen, and a number of other Renton women who helped out. Those were the days we worked 14 or 15 hours a day.

The problem was greater than the loss of a few short-order cooks. Literally thousands of

With B-29 Superfortress airplanes as a backdrop, the Boeing choral group tries to lift wartime Christmas spirits at the Renton Boeing plant in 1944. Courtesy, Renton Historical Society and Museum

One of Pacific Car and Foundry's important contributions to the wartime effort was the construction of formidible Sherman tanks. Courtesy, Renton Historical Society and Museum

workers were needed, and those that could not be found locally had to be brought in from out of state. The federal government helped the community cope with explosive growth, building a new fire station in 1942 and a new hospital a year later. To accommodate the thousands of new workers and their families, it built and administered immense housing projects, among them the Highlands, east of Renton, and Cedar River Park. To accommodate the influx of schoolchildren, it built a new school in the Highlands, staying barely ahead of the flood of children in the fall of 1943 by putting up two new classrooms every week. It also built a war production school to train workers in the skills needed to operate the plants.

There was prosperity, surely, but it was too much, too fast. Concerns about how their community was faring and how it would cope with the changes sure to come when the war ended prompted several businessmen to organize the Renton Rotary Club in 1943, to provide a place where they could compare notes and share ideas. In the milling press of humanity, the town struggled to keep from coming apart; struggled to cope with wartime blackouts, rationing, swingshifts and graveyard shifts; struggled with children left alone while their mothers worked; and struggled with people from other parts of the country whom locals did not understand and who did not understand them. When the war finally did end on September 2, 1945, everyone rejoiced and breathed a sigh of relief. It was over. Maybe, now, things could get back to normal. But by then the definition of normalcy had changed.

The USO sponsored knitting classes for young women, encouraging them to help in the war effort by knitting clothing for the men overseas. Courtesy, Renton Historical Society and Museum

CHAPTER 6

Meeting Modern Challenges

This circa 1956 promotional Boeing photograph features a KC-135, constructed at the Renton plant, soaring past Mount Rainier. Courtesy, The Boeing Company

At the end of the war, Renton faced all the problems of a modern city: overcrowding, a fast pace, and a sense of anonymity among its citizens. Fortunately the task of transforming an inflated, disparate population into a community was a familiar one, and the work was taken up by the same institutions: the schools, churches, clubs, and community organizations that nurtured a sense of belonging and a cooperative effort.

Most of Renton's newer citizens lived in the housing projects, 10,000 of them in the Highlands alone. The Highland's 2,500 houses included many permanent single family dwellings but also a large number of temporary duplexes and fourplexes. Residents worked to make their homes neat and attractive, but found it difficult to keep things clean. Houses were heated with

The Kiwanis Club sponsored many community efforts, including the drive to build a public swimming pool in 1947. Ed Shearer poses with the airplane that was used for promotional flights over the city. Courtesy, Renton Historical Society and Museum

coal and with rubber scraps taken from a huge tire dump, so dust blackened driveways and thick smoke fouled the air and covered everything with a thin film of soot. The permanent houses were sturdily built, but the sameness of their design presented a numbing anonymity, which to some characterized life itself in the projects. One man who grew up in the Highlands observed that, "it was never a community—just houses."

Others felt differently. Many of the black Americans who moved to Renton during and after the war lived in the projects because the rents were low and because they were not welcomed in other neighborhoods. A strong sense of community developed that was celebrated years later at large neighborhood picnics. Some joined with other black families who had already been living here to become part of the Renton Full Gospel Pentecostal Federated Church in Kennydale.

The projects housed people from all over the country, and the chaos of wartime inspired a certain amount of hell-raising, particularly among single men. Police Chief Clarence Williams, who began work as an officer in Renton in 1944, recalled, "A great many of Boeing's new employees came from small towns, particularly those in the South. They had never worked in a large plant before; they knew nothing about life in a large town or city." Williams added, "We had the usual trouble with young people in the new housing units at Cedar River Park."

The latter phenomenon, a local manifestation of a national epidemic of juvenile delinquency during and after the war, was examined in an article in *Life* magazine titled "Renton's Juvenile Wolf Packs" that caused many residents to cringe.

If the region faced significant problems, it also demonstrated the ability to deal with them. A solid community spirit developed in

RIGHT: Employees in industries that were not directly tied to military products experienced a smoother transition as Renton adapted to postwar economic conditions. In 1949, Gladding McBean employees pose under their company sign, which advertises available positions. Courtesy, Renton Historical Society and Museum

When production slowed down at the end of World War II, Boeing property became a vast storage facility for surplus military inventory. Courtesy, Renton Historical Society and Museum

the Highlands based largely on the efforts of Pastor William Wilson and his wife, Inez, graduates of the Multnomah School of the Bible in Portland, Oregon. They had organized Bible classes in Maple Valley after the war and were asked to take up the work begun by the Renton Ministerial Association, which had tried, unsuccessfully, to develop a Highlands congregation. The Wilsons involved themselves in youth work among the throngs of children living in the community, organizing vacation Bible schools that featured parades down local streets. Out of these programs, and with support from a half-dozen adults, they created the Highlands Community Church. Formally organized in 1950, it was the first church in the Highlands, and soon one of the largest in Renton.

The need for youth programs prompted the Lions Club to bring the Renton Rodeo back for another season, and to build a youth camp on land along the Cedar River deeded to the Lions in 1946. That same year, voters approved a bond issue enabling the school district to construct a large athletic stadium near the high school. A year later the district purchased the Tonelli farm beside the Cedar River for use as an athletic field and worked to ready it for the 1948 fall football season. In 1947 the Kiwanis Club sent past-president Ed Shearer aloft in a small plane over town to broadcast an appeal for voters to approve a construction bond for a municipal swimming pool. The bond passed, and the next year the pool was built. Shortly afterward Kiwanians spearheaded efforts to develop Kiwanis Park in the Highlands.

Youth was much on the minds of school officials who foresaw the impact of the "baby boom" sired by millions of servicemen returning

In a spectacular postwar deal, the City of Renton was able to purchase the airport from the federal government for the price of one dollar. Mayor Perry Mitchell officially accepts the title to the Renton Airport in 1946. Courtesy, Renton Historical Society and Museum

home from the war. In the interest of efficiency, voters in 1942 had approved the merger of the Renton School District with six other outlying districts. During the war the resources of the new district were stretched to the limit, and peace brought no respite. In fact, enrollment grew at a faster rate after the war than during it. Responding to the challenge, voters regularly approved bonds for the construction of additions to buildings and for new schools, beginning with Skyway Elementary School in 1948.

Many feared that the postwar economic slump, forecast as servicemen flooded the job market and industries retooled for peacetime production, would be severe and long lasting. Fighting had barely halted when Boeing announced it would lay off 8,000 workers at its Renton plant. Work on the last of the B-29s continued until May 1946, but gradually the huge government-owned buildings fell silent, and for a while they were used to store surplus navy flying boats. There were also cutbacks at Pacific Car and Foundry as sales, which had totaled $50 million in 1945, shrank to $19.4 million in 1946.

Nevertheless, the economic calamity these developments portended never occurred. The slowdown at the major plants was only temporary, and more than offset by rapid growth in construction, retail sales, and services. The huge influx of people into western Washington during the war created a large market for goods, and the demand for consumer products, suppressed by depression and war, once released generated a postwar boom.

In spite of the social problems that accompanied its wartime transformation, Renton prospered. The federal government pumped nearly $4 million into housing and $300,000 into street improvements. Federal funds helped Renton upgrade and expand its water and

The sons and daughters of some of Renton's pioneers gather for a quick snapshot in 1944. In this close-knit community, the children of established friends often grew up to become friends themselves. Courtesy, Renton Historical Society and Museum

The impressive Dash-80 aircraft, the first of the jet-powered planes to be built at Boeing's Renton plant, was rolled out to the applause of the public in 1954. Courtesy, The Boeing Company

sewer systems, and provided $250,000 worth of machine equipment to the school district's vocational education program. After the war, administration of the Highlands and Cedar River Park projects was turned over to the City of Renton, and the federal government sold the vastly improved airport to the city for one dollar. The city moved its municipal offices into the vacated Cedar River Park Project Administration Building, and in 1948 local citizens purchased Renton Hospital from the government for a fraction of its construction costs.

Moreover, federal investments at Pacific Car and Foundry and Boeing paid off handsomely once manufacturing in those plants regained momentum. Orders for Pacific Car's prewar specialty, refrigerated boxcars, skyrocketed. The company recaptured its winch market, and its Structural Steel Division experienced unprecedented demand as construction in the Northwest boomed. The Renton plant was also hard at work building school buses—a portent of future growth—until that job was turned over to the recently acquired Kenworth Motor Truck Corporation in Seattle. At Boeing work got underway in 1948 on the production of KC-97 Stratofreighters and Stratotankers, the first of more than 800 assembled at Renton.

Because an educated and well-trained work force was in these companies' interest, they vigorously supported schools. The taxes companies paid and the monies still coming in from the federal government kept residential property taxes low enough to sustain popular enthusiasm for social and civic improvements. Local support of the schools also derived from the solid working-class character of the community. Hard work was considered a virtue as well as a fact of life, and the benefits of an education were immediately apparent in wage scales with unskilled laborers at the bottom, skilled workers in the middle, and managers and professionals in possession of high school and college diplomas at the top.

Health care was another much appreciated item, and Renton's citizens pioneered a novel form of hospital funding by creating the first public hospital district in the state. The Federal Works Administration had built Renton Hospital, whose seven wings converged onto a central hub like the spokes of a wheel, for $750,000, and during the war a locally elected administrative group leased it from the government. When it was designated surplus property after the war, the community sought to purchase the hospital outright. Fortunately the state legislature provided the means by passing legislation that enabled voters to create public hospital districts. Revenue from moderate property tax assessments in a district could be used to build or purchase a hospital and help maintain it.

In Renton the district's boundaries were drawn to follow closely those of the school district, and in November 1947, on one of the rainiest days of the year, voters within the proposed Public Hospital District No. 1 voted overwhelmingly for the plan. "I thought," said one woman, "it was more important than voting for the president." On January 1, 1948, the district became a reality, and in September Renton Hospital was purchased from the government for $200,000.

After Bronson Hospital closed in 1952, Renton Hospital became the area's major care unit, and it was always busy. Dr. S. John Vukov, who started practicing in Renton in 1940, recalled that during his stay at the hospital he delivered more babies than there were people in the city when he arrived.

The 1950 census count of 16,039 people in Renton demonstrated that most of those who came during the Second World War had liked it well enough to stay. Jobs were plentiful during the Korean War as industries filled Defense Department contracts. In Renton, Pacific Car and Foundry developed and produced the T-87 and T-108 self-propelled guns and worked on an amphibious assault vehicle for the navy. Boeing increased its production of Stratofreighters, but in a walled-off section of the plant, work went forward on a revolutionary new aircraft.

Jet engines had already made propeller-driven, long-range bombers obsolete, and the company's success with its jet-powered B-47 bomber indicated the time was ripe to develop a commercial jet aircraft. In 1952 Boeing decided to gamble $16 million—nearly all its potential capital—and build a prototype for a jet transport.

Work went on in secret in Renton, and part by part an impressively sleek and swept-wing craft took shape. In little more than two years the new aircraft, designated the 367-80 or "Dash-80," was completed. On May 15, 1954, the magnificent four-engined jet, with its yellow top and copper-brown trim, was rolled out of the plant for its first public appearance, an event that received broad national and international coverage.

This Boeing aircraft, sporting a United Airlines logo, proudly bears the name of the "City of Renton." Courtesy, Renton Historical Society and Museum

Two months later the aircraft that aeronautical historians describe as one of the most important ever built was ready for its test flight. It was an extraordinary moment. The company's future depended on the Dash-80's performance, and as test pilot Tex Johnston and copilot Dex

Loesch were about to enter the plane, company president William Allen gripped Johnston's arm. "How do you feel?" he asked. "Never better," Johnston replied. Allen then bid them on: "She's in your hands, boys. Good luck."

In the cockpit Johnston and Loesch powered the plane up and taxied to its takeoff position. With engines at full throttle, the Dash-80 moved down the runway, slowly at first, then picking up speed until, after what to observers seemed an awfully long time, the nose lifted and the future of commercial aviation, of Boeing, and of Renton itself, ascended gracefully into the bright Northwestern air.

The water took wing that day. The Dash-80 began its epic flight near the old confluence of the lake outlet and the Cedar River, where the *skai-TAW* promised wealth to those who would wrestle with it. Where Duwamish women pried wapato bulbs from the warm mud, a struggle for knowledge and power, inflamed by war, released a graceful, powerful new creature from the dead river's cradle and gave birth to the jet age. This was Renton's child, built in Renton by many who had been born in its hospitals and educated in its schools.

Although it was a long time before airlines were persuaded to buy its new bird, Boeing would enjoy phenomenal success. In July 1956 the last propeller-driven KC-97 Stratofreighter was towed out of the plant, and the first production model of the new KC-135 jet transport, christened "City of Renton," was introduced to the world. Two years later the first airliner version of the Dash-80, the Boeing 707, was towed to its parking stall beside the huge new assembly building, the first of many to come.

A row of aircraft is checked at Boeing's plant in Renton. Photo by Eric Draper

Roadways which cross over the Cedar River have helped to ease the traffic into downtown Renton. Photo by Eric Draper

By then Renton was edging toward its 1960 census count of 18,453. The town itself had expanded far beyond its original boundaries as outlying districts petitioned the city for annexation. Because of Renton's broad tax base, property owners near town found it cheaper to obtain utilities and services by joining the city than by joining local cooperatives or obtaining them from the county. As a result, the city limits had expanded to the lake and spread out beyond Earlington and the Highlands and toward Longacres, active once again after being used as an artillery stockade during the war. The business district had expanded from Third Avenue to Second and Fourth avenues, and businesses proliferated along the arterials converging upon the city.

Calling itself the "Hub City of Enterprise," Renton had become one of the most important manufacturing centers in the state. Boeing was by far the largest company, employing 35,000 workers in its Renton and Seattle plants in 1954, placing it head, shoulders, hips, and knees above any other manufacturer. Pacific Car and Foundry was a strong second, however.

Gladding McBean continued to manufacture facing brick and ceramic pipe, and two coal mines still produced at modest levels. Several lumber mills maintained operations along the lakeshore. In addition Renton produced cement; it also had a meat packing plant, and the Spider Staging Company manufactured a unique self-raising scaffold. Root beer was produced at A.H. Rutherford & Sons Triple X plant, and their drive-in restaurants became commonplace in the region. One of the newer industries to come to Renton in the late 1950s was a cardboard box fabrication plant built by the American Container Corporation.

Renton supported two newspapers, the biweekly *Renton Chronicle* and the weekly *Renton News-Record,* and in 1947 it had its own radio station, KLAN, broadcasting what it termed a "middle of the road" music selection. On Saturday nights the station broadcast a local auction, and during the pre-Easter season it sponsored rabbit races to attract shoppers downtown.

Downtown needed some attraction. Buildings 20 and 30 years old were showing their age, and the narrow downtown streets were often jammed with automobiles. Worse, places to park were scarce.

Increasingly, with more cars and better roads, people found it convenient to drive miles from their homes to do "one-stop shopping" at places where parking was ample and free. The success of the Northgate Shopping Center in Seattle and Bellevue Square in Bellevue pointed the way to the future, and Renton real estate agent Robert Edwards followed suit. In 1952 he had purchased the field where Erasmus Smithers had pastured his milk cows, but the land's value did not rise as he had hoped. His luck turned, however, when a representative of Sears Roebuck & Company asked if he would be willing to build a new Sears store on it and surround it with smaller retail stores. In October 1960 Edwards opened the Renton Shopping Center fronting Rainier Avenue, and Renton had its first shopping mall surrounded by acres of parking.

Along with nearby Renton Village and the Highlands Shopping Center, these malls succeeded in attracting shoppers to Renton. When the new Southcenter Mall opened in Tukwila in the mid-1960s, patronage at the Renton Shopping Center dwindled, but eventually returned to and surpassed the earlier level. But the success of the outlying centers helped drain the life from the old business district, once the heart of town.

Renton, which had been surrounded by farms, forests, and failed company towns, now found itself competing with vigorous new suburban communities. To the south, Kent awakened from its rural slumber and spread in all directions. To the west, Tukwila boomed. But the real phenomenon was Bellevue on the first floating bridge, which had diverted traffic from the old Sunset Highway route through Renton. When Bellevue was incorporated in 1953, it had 5,950 people. In 1960 the population grew to 12,809, and 10 years later, after many annexations, it mushroomed to more than 60,000.

The communities east and south of Lake Washington were linked together by Highway 405, built in the early 1960s. The highway joined the new Interstate 5 south at Tukwila and was connected to Seattle via the new Evergreen Point Floating Bridge constructed north of Bellevue. In Renton engineers avoided downtown by building along the brow of Renton Hill, but the twists and turns this required produced the notorious "S" curves. During rush hours, slowdowns on these curves caused traffic jams, and when road conditions were poor they were the scenes of innumerable wrecks.

Businessmen complained that the placement of exits north and south of town discouraged commerce. When the state refused to redesign the North Renton freeway interchange to give Boeing and Pacific Car and Foundry workers easier access to their plants, local voters, with the leadership of the Greater Renton Chamber of Commerce, passed a $400,000 bond to have the necessary work done.

Actually, the placement of the interchanges may have saved the old center of town from destruction, but to thrive again it needed more customers. City planners had several plans drawn up to rejuvenate the area, to block off traffic and create a pedestrian mall, but railroad right-of-ways complicated efforts, and many worried that blocking off streets would only make already complex traffic patterns worse.

In spite of these problems Renton continued to grow. Between 1950 and 1960 the school district built seven new elementary schools and started an eighth; it also built two new middle schools and added classrooms and portables to older buildings. In the early 1960s schools could not be built fast enough to keep up with enrollment, and there was double shifting in some buildings as there had been during World War II.

The growth of the district was accompanied by a worrisome trend. As the federal government sold its holdings to corporations, the city, and private individuals, the amount it contributed to the community in lieu of taxes declined, and the local tax burden increased. In addition, the percentage of property tax paid by individual property owners increased, and that paid by large corporations such as Boeing,

The staff of Renton's city government poses for a group portrait in 1964. Courtesy, Renton Historical Society and Museum

Pacific Car and Foundry, and Puget Power declined. More and more, people began to feel the bite of taxes.

Under the long superintendency of Oliver Hazen, the school district had enjoyed general public support for its expenditures. Yet after he retired in 1966, modifications in the way courses were taught, controversial changes in curriculum, and increasing costs began to inspire citizen protests.

These protests were muted, however, as Boeing increased production of its 707 jetliners and began building its new 727 and 737 models. More workers were hired, a new plant opened in Auburn, and by 1969 the student population in the Renton school district peaked at 16,123, a 700 percent increase since World War II.

The unique Renton Public Library spans the Cedar River. Photo by Eric Draper

The city itself planned a new civic center and began by building a new, river-spanning library. The old Carnegie library had long outlived its usefulness, but debate over the location and cost of a replacement resulted in voter defeat of three successive bond issues. During a subsequent city council meeting in 1964, someone jested that the land problem could be solved if the new library was built over the river. The joke was taken seriously, however, and a local architectural firm was asked to draw up a plan for such a structure. Voters liked the idea well enough to approve the construction bond, and the building soon took wing above the river.

When it was dedicated in April 1966 the building was a local hit and a regional triumph, and it revived interest in Renton's past. While construction was still underway, librarian Marcella Hillgen set up a historical committee to organize a display of photographs and memorabilia collected by a citizens group, Friends of the Library. The enthusiasm inspired by the display convinced members that more work was needed to preserve and celebrate Renton's history, and the Renton Historical Society was organized to carry out the work.

In 1968 a new, six-story city hall rose beside the river near the site of the old library, and in 1969 the Pacific Car and Foundry Foundation awarded the city a $100,000 grant for the creation of a performing arts center. The city contributed an equal share; a site at Cedar River Park was selected, and in 1970 construction of the new Carco Theater began.

As the civic center was taking shape, it became obvious that Renton Hospital's location—near an ever-busier airport and next to a major highway—was unsuitable. Because of this and other shortcomings, the United States Department of Public Health declared in a 1964 report that the facility was "permanently unusable." Hospital district administrators had purchased land for a new building in the Highlands, but when it was learned that groups in Kent were planning to create a hospital district of their own, a move that would have drained revenue from Renton's, another site farther south was purchased. Acrimony over the costly switch and other issues dogged officials' efforts, but in 1966 voters approved a bond to build a hospital on the new site, and in October 1969 Valley General Hospital, the most modern and comprehensive health care facility in the area, opened its doors.

Citizens demonstrated a well-earned pride in these accomplishments, but with the advent of the 1970s they became increasingly apprehensive. In the summer of 1968 Boeing, which employed more than 104,000 people in the

Seattle-Renton area, was gearing up for a new project as momentous—and risky—as the development of the Dash-80. This was the Supersonic Transport, or SST, a huge aircraft designed to go more than twice the speed of sound, a project whose success depended upon substantial federal funding. At the time Boeing was plagued by a near-total collapse of commercial orders and a downturn in Vietnam war purchases, and was burdened with start-up costs for production of the 747 jumbo jet.

When Congress voted not to fund the SST, Boeing cut its employment by two-thirds in a single year. The layoffs produced a severe local recession, cushioned somewhat in Renton where the production of other jetliners continued. Nevertheless the city's population declined slightly during 1971 and 1972.

However slight, this decline had a severe impact upon the school district. By 1971, nine new elementary schools, a new middle school, and two new high schools, Hazen and Lindbergh, had been added to the list of those already built. An entirely new Vocational Technical School campus had been built in the Highlands, a new administration building had been completed, and the district was $3 million in debt. The natural drop in enrollment that came with the aging of the baby boom added to the lost population, resulting in classrooms only recently completed now being left empty. Adding to the district's problems was community uproar over a sex education program newly introduced into the curriculum and dissension between teachers and administrators over contract issues.

The modernistic Renton Municipal Building was constructed in 1968 near the site of the old library. Photo by Eric Draper

In 1971 a school levy was defeated by Renton voters—the first levy defeat in Renton's history. Without money to pay them, over 100 teachers were laid off. Lawsuits were filed against the district, teachers went on strike, the school board dismissed the superintendent, and he in turn sued the board. Enrollments continued to fall, and the rancor of dispute hung over the district like a sullen cloud.

The problems afflicting the schools reflected those troubling the broader community. Many feared changes they could not control. In 1974 *Seattle Post Intelligencer* writer Richard Hardesty summed up the situation in Renton: "Renton is a working-class town, fragmented by its shopping center—subdivision communities, with no central leadership able to speak for the citizens as a whole, and dependent for its economic life on

LEFT: Though plagued with problems in the early 1970s, the Renton School District has overcome its difficulties and continues to provide a solid education for the area's children. Photo by Eric Draper

The Renton Historical Museum now occupies the old fire station which was originally built under the WPA in the 1930s. The three main bays have been restored as exhibit and display areas. Courtesy, Renton Historical Society and Museum

Boeing and Pacific Car and Foundry."

It was a harsh assessment, and it suggested that Renton had become what it had never been before, a company town. Many citizens resented the fact that those who owned and managed the companies the city depended on lived in Seattle or Bellevue. Renton's citizens might wear the badge of a "blue-collar town" with stubborn pride, but many white-collar professionals did not find the label attractive. Their fathers may have been blue collar, but hadn't they worked hard so their children wouldn't have to?

Renton was not glamorous. While new tract homes had sprouted in its outlying districts like weeds, the city's central core and older neighborhoods were threatened with decay. And as the people buying those new houses spent fewer years living in them as they moved from job to job, their ties to place—ties that inspired community improvement—were weakened. But life had never been especially easy in Renton, and as they had before, people rose to the challenge.

Fortunately, the recession was short-lived. During the 1970s Renton's population grew from 25,000 to more than 30,000. While the nation celebrated its bicentennial, Renton could boast more than 100 manufacturing firms producing everything from jet planes and railroad cars to coiled springs and plastics. Economically the city was healthy, and it had taken pains to make itself more attractive. Under the directorship of Gene Coulon, the city parks system had been upgraded and expanded. Green belts were preserved, the banks of the Commercial Waterway were beautified, and a magnificent new park, the Gene Coulon Memorial Park, was developed along the lakeshore.

During the bicentennial the community

The Wilson family helped to establish the Highlands Community Church in 1950, which now houses one of the largest congregations in Renton. Photo by Eric Draper

LEFT: A father and son enjoy an afternoon of play at Liberty Park. Photo by Eric Draper

created a permanent historical museum in the old WPA fire station. The collection begun in the new library had spent several years in rooms in the old Highlands administration building. However, when a new fire station was built next to the old one, the city donated it to the historical society, which restored the building and developed comprehensive displays examining Renton's history. With a $3,000 grant from the Renton Rotary, the society also published the first detailed history of the community, *Renton: From Coal to Jets,* by local journalist and writer Morda Slauson.

Both the museum and the book represented a significant effort to preserve and celebrate the city's heritage and identity. A city is more than just houses, buildings, and factories. It is first a community, and a community needs more than bread alone to live. It also needs a sense of itself as a place where the hopes and dreams of individuals can soar. To the extent it is that kind of place, it will prosper.

A dream of the first people, the Duwamish, came alive in 1979 when archaeologists digging across from the Renton Shopping Center unearthed a longhouse floor at the old village site at *Sbah-bah-DEED.* The remains of this and of a much older longhouse unearthed farther down the old Black River channel called to mind the fact that people had lived and prospered here for centuries.

In recent times, however, the Duwamish had not fared well. When Henry Moses, the last of the Renton chiefs, died in January 1969, it seemed an important link with Renton's native past was broken. The famous 1974 Boldt decision reaffirming native treaty rights to half the salmon catch did not apply to the modern Duwamish because the government did not recognize them as a separate tribe. Hundreds of Duwamish who could demonstrate identification with other recognized tribes did so, and the tribal roll shrank from approximately 1,100 to 300.

Still, the remaining Duwamish persevered. Friends reached out to them in 1976 when the city named its municipal pool after Henry Moses, and then came the excavations of 1979 and the early 1980s. These excavations inspired a vision of a cultural center where the artifacts that had been recovered could be displayed to reaffirm the Duwamish peoples' presence in the wonderful place that had been, and still is, their home.

It was Barbara Shinpoch's dream to become Renton's first woman mayor, and in 1979 she won the election with the help of dedicated friends and family members. Her husband, A.N. "Bud" Shinpoch, was a well-regarded state senator, and for 24 years she had served on a variety of boards and committees in the commu-

Summertime brings a chance to play in Carco Park and to swim in the many swimming areas of the Cedar River, activities which have been enjoyed by generations of Renton citizens. Courtesy, Renton Historical Society and Museum

OPPOSITE: Stately Mount Rainier peeks over the greenery surrounding Lake Desire. Photo by Gary Greene

nity and had sat on the city council. When critics wondered whether a middle-aged woman was up to the job of mayor, she answered in a speech titled, "How to Manage a City and Hot Flashes at the Same Time," which drew delighted applause at several womens' social and professional clubs. Her two successful terms as mayor in an era of reduced expectations were marked by pragmatism, strong citizen involvement, and good humor, qualities that had always served Renton well.

When she turned over her gavel to her successor, Earl Clymer, in 1988, she left him a city fiscally sound and with enhanced services and stronger ties to neighboring communities. Clymer, a descendent of early settler Christian Clymer, noted in his first state of the city speech that the value of construction permits issued that year, totaling $150 million, was the largest in Renton's history. He also observed that coping with accelerating growth presented the city with its greatest challenge.

Like most cities, Renton faces a future full of problems and opportunities. The brick factory has gone the way of other industries; Pacific Car and Foundry (PACCAR since 1972) is moving out—but might be replaced by the Kenworth Truck Manufacturing Company; and Boeing is expanding production to meet increasing demand. Although Renton is sometimes described as a company town or as a bedroom community, its economy is too complex for it to be thus caricatured. Despite the huge economic shadow cast by Boeing, despite the fact that the city includes a jet in its logo, it is no more a company town now than it was when coal was king. When the last mines shut down, citizens marked their closure as the end of an era, not that of the town, and when the last Boeing jet rolls from the plant—rendered obsolete by some new technology—Renton will in all likelihood be around to mark that passing and continue on.

What it will be then is anyone's guess. The small town that became a city at the end of the war is now so interdependent with its neighbors that it is an integral part of something larger. There is no agreement yet about what that larger something is called: Greater Seattle or Metropolitan King County, Megalopolis, or Slurb, but whatever it is, Renton is part of it. The freeways and their rushing traffic are only the most visible signs of the ties that bind the whole together.

Like that of the rest of the region, Renton's economy is moving into the realm of high-tech industry. Its excellent location, served by major highway, air, and rail connections, continues to attract investment. Increasingly, older warehouses are being replaced by gleaming office complexes, hotels, and motels. New annexations promise the addition of 20,000 citizens to the city's rolls, and its commerce will benefit by the completion of the extensive new Orillia Shopping Center.

But the pressure to build has not come at the expense of Renton's livability. Handsome older buildings such as the old Puget Sound Power and Light Substation, the city's first all-brick building, and the Milwaukee Road substation have been preserved and restored for modern use. As new homes, apartments, and condominiums are built in ouytlying districts, the graceful older homes nearer the heart of town are being restored. More parkland is being purchased, and soon walkers will be able to follow a footpath from the mouth of the Cedar River to the Maplewood golf course several miles upstream. Up the hill, in the Greenwood Memorial Park, the grave of rock star Jimi Hendrix has become a kind of shrine, attracting devotees locally and from countries around the world. The route along the river will take walkers past modern industrial plants to habitats as green as when Henry Tobin staked his claim.

Ultimately, Renton's future will lie in the hands of its people. A common thread that runs through its history is that most of those who came here stayed. They found it a wonderful place, and they fought to keep—and worked to make—it so. Doubtless their efforts will continue, because they are motivated by a deep love of abiding things. These things are best understood if we return to the library that spans the river and listen to the water moving beneath the shade of the trees. The splashing of fish swimming upstream to spawn are joined by the shouts of children playing in the swimming pool and in the playground, rising on swings so high it seems they could touch the sky with their toes.

It is a wonderful place. It is a place where dreams as well as water can take wing.

ABOVE: A crowd of spectators watches an exciting race at the Longacres Racetrack. Photo by Gary Greene

RIGHT: A young boy and his grandfather walk hand in hand at the Gene Coulon Memorial Park. Photo by Eric Draper

OPPOSITE, TOP: Windsurfing along the waters of Lake Washington is one of the many water sports to be enjoyed in the Renton area. Photo by Eric Draper

OPPOSITE, BOTTOM: This skateboarder executes a thrilling leap into the air in downtown Renton. Photo by Eric Draper

LEFT: The Cedar River is a popular place to cool off during the hot summer months. Photo by Eric Draper

TOP: Children and adults can experience "Interface," a lively bronze sculpture located at Gene Coulon Memorial Park. Photo by Eric Draper

ABOVE: Rainier Avenue South in the heart of Renton bustles with evening activity. Photo by Eric Draper

RIGHT: An airplane takes off into the sunset from the Renton Airport. Photo by Eric Draper

OPPOSITE: A spectacular sunset illuminates the waters of Lake Washington. Photo by Gary Greene

BELOW: Gene Coulon Beach Park serves as one of the most popular recreation spots in the Renton area and provides a lunchtime escape for local workers. Photo by Gary Greene

CHAPTER 7

Partners in Progress

Logging and lumber interests in early Renton were represented by the fraternal organization of the Modern Woodsmen of the World. Courtesy, Renton Historical Society and Museum

Renton, like so many other small towns that grew into thriving communities, has its roots in a multifaceted base. Early economic foundations, such as mining and transportation, were expanded upon by the pioneers of the area to turn what was scarcely a wide spot in the road into a vital small town, bustling with energy and vision for the future.

Many businesses operating today in Renton have their roots in those early years of the community. Also, since many businesses in Renton have been family concerns over several generations, and since their founders and owners have directly participated in the growth of the area, the title "Partners in Progress" truly applies. These pioneer families and businesses have helped to shape and mold Renton since its inception, and their influence is very much present today.

As important as these early pioneers have been, the face and destiny of Renton was also shaped by the cataclysmic force of World War II. Renton was a thriving small town of fewer than 5,000 people at the beginning of the war, but the almost instantaneous demand for goods and services to support the war effort swelled the population overnight, which placed a tremendous demand on the community. Some pioneer businesses changed the focus of their efforts and began making products for the war effort. Other business sprang up to provide the necessities of life for the burgeoning population that came to the area to work in the wartime-related industries. Still other community-support services, such as hospitals, had to increase their facilities immediately to meet the demands of the population growth.

Many of the people who came to Renton to work in the wartime industries remained after the war and decided to call Renton their home. In addition, former Renton residents returning from the war settled in their hometown and began business ventures. Renton, which had been changed forever by World War II, had that change solidified in the years after the war as both the newcomers and the natives worked together to encourage the continued growth and stability of the community.

In recent years Renton businesses have extended their horizons to encompass ever-increasing international trade with the effect of further strengthening the community. Pioneers, wartime entrepreneurs, and new businesspeople have joined together as Partners in Progress in their determination to help their community's continued development.

The organizations whose stories are detailed on the following pages have chosen to support this important literary and civic project. They illustrate the varied ways in which individuals and businesses have contributed to the area's growth and development. Their stories reveal the hard work, commitment, and vision of Renton's citizens, who have made Renton an excellent place to live and work.

GREATER RENTON CHAMBER OF COMMERCE

An account published in the April 11, 1912, edition of the *Renton Herald* informed the community the "Commercial Club" had been organized to "unite all those who have the best interest of the city at heart and to work for the proper development of the town." This statement, made so long ago by those who organized the Commercial Club for the benefit of the Renton community, is remarkably similar to the current purpose statement of the Commercial Club's successor, the Greater Renton Chamber of Commerce, which emphasizes the joining together of the area's "business and professional people" to improve "the conditions under which commercial, industrial, educational, civic, and socioeconomic growth are conducted . . ."

Interest in the future development of the Renton community began early as the 1910 brochure entitled *Renton: The City of Great Possibilities* outlined the area's virtues, especially its "tremendous industrial future," and the emphasis on Renton's suitability for development continued throughout the club's early years as the area's growing coal-mining operation began to attract other industries.

The Commercial Club became the Renton Chamber of Commerce in 1919, and from that time until 1945 the organization was run on a volunteer basis with a president and a board of directors who set and implemented policy and raised funds. In 1946 then-president Charlie McGarrigle hired the chamber's first manager, Henry Reynolds, who held that position until 1962. One of McGarrigle's favorite stories—he is still active in the chamber today, selling members—is that when the organization ran out of funds to pay Henry's salary, members would sell a piano, chair, or any piece of equipment the chamber could do without. Kay F. Johnson, the chamber's current manager, was hired and began work on February 15, 1962.

In 1961 the Greater Renton Chamber of Commerce rallied behind the construction of the new chamber building. Pictured (from left) are Ned Stokes, chairman; Orrin K. Moody; Henry Reynolds, chamber manager; Stan Wagner; Sam Cayce; Bev Morrison; Swede Koenigs; John Swanson; Hayden Williams; Joe Gerber; and Robert H. Moffat. On the committee but not in the picture were Bill Hazelett, Glenn Wallin, Oliver Hazen, and Howard M. Shaw.

With the shift to the manager form of organization came a change in the operation of the chamber. The board of directors still set policies, but it became the manager's job to see that those policies were implemented. Another of the manager's duties was to raise needed finances.

In 1961 the chamber was successful in raising the money needed to construct its present offices at 300 Rainier Avenue North, and, with donated labor and materials, the building was erected. The facility was remodeled in the late 1970s.

At present, in addition to a manager, a board of directors composed of volunteers, and a president, the chamber has several permanent committees set up to deal with various aspects of its operations and to address special problems or projects. Among the chamber's objectives is the goal of providing leadership to help solve community problems, and the committees aid in fulfilling this goal.

The organization also seeks to serve to coordinate efforts to strengthen the business climate while creating a broad base of participation within the Renton community and to facilitate understanding of and appreciation for the free enterprise system. In addition, the Greater Renton Chamber of Commerce has completed a 15-year accreditation program that consists of a self-evaluation process overseen by the Chamber of Commerce of the United States. Achievement of this accreditation certifies that the Greater Renton Chamber of Commerce can create and implement a suitable plan of action to meet its stated goals of improving the business climate and promoting the city's growth.

Remodeling was completed on the new chamber building in 1979, and refurbishing of the entire building was begun in 1988.

BEADEX

The original Beadex building was located at 4615 Eighth Avenue Northwest in Seattle and was occupied by the company until it moved to Renton in 1972. It featured a large, distinctive sign that was a landmark in the community. Courtesy, Margaret Campbell

In 1947 Seattle inventor Art Dunlop developed a product that revolutionized the drywall industry. Dunlop invented a corner protecting bead for wallboard, as well as the machinery to produce the bead, and patented the whole process in 1948 under the name of Beadex. That year he founded the now Renton-based company of the same name.

Dunlop first began the Beadex operations in Ballard; when he opened the plant the five employees produced 15,000 feet of bead per day by hand. Demand for the product, which featured paper laminated over the metal corner bead and allowed easy painting and nail-free application, was so great that the plant could hardly keep up with orders. As Dunlop refined the necessary machinery to manufacture the bead, the business grew.

Dunlop was, however, an entrepreneur with varying interests, and in 1964 he sold Beadex to his nephew, William Campbell. Campbell, described by those who knew him as a dedicated businessman with an excellent reputation in the drywall industry, worked hard to build up the operation, and it prospered under his leadership. Campbell, who was well known for his policy of quality and service, expanded the product line and introduced joint compounds.

In 1972 Campbell moved Beadex to its current Renton location, and the process of manufacturing the bead changed a little. Different shapes and designs were made, and modern, hot-melt gluing systems were employed.

While on a business trip in 1976, Campbell suffered a fatal heart attack. Following his death, his wife, Margaret, ran Beadex as its president until she sold the company in 1981 to Ken Kelly. Kelly's tenure as president was only for a year as the firm again was sold, this time to The Synkoloid Company of Canada. In 1987 Beadex ownership changed again to its current owner, CSR Overseas Investments, Ltd., of Sydney, Australia.

According to Don King, who came to Beadex seven years ago as a general manager and is now the president, the company ships its products internationally as well as throughout the United States. Today, to keep up with orders, five workers can produce 200,000 feet of bead per day. The firm has also grown in terms of plant sites during the past three years. There are manufacturing plants in Stockton and Riverside, California, which employ 22 and 25 people, respectively, and a distribution center in Portland, Oregon, with two employees.

Beadex has been a contributing member of the community and currently employs 44 people at its Renton plant. In addition, it is a member of the Greater Renton Chamber of Commerce and participates in the Renton Slo-Pitch Softball League.

Art Dunlop, inventor and entrepreneur, developed a corner protecting bead that completely changed the drywall industry and led to the formation of the Beadex company. Courtesy, Margaret Campbell

THE BOEING COMPANY

In 1941 the small 4,000-person community of Renton was selected as the site of a new government defense plant to manufacture airplanes. It was a momentus decision because in a short time nearly 8,000 Boeing workers arrived, and Renton was set on a course to become the Jet Capital of the World.

Although abrupt, the change had been years in the making. Shortly before World War I in 1916 William E. Boeing, a timber dealer, established an airplane company in Seattle that produced naval training planes. The company became a very successful builder of fighter planes during the next decade. It then moved into the market for large military and commercial airplanes in the 1930s. As World War II approached, the need for more floor space brought about a decision to build a huge new plant.

Renton's construction added 2.2 million square feet of floor space by the time of its completion in June 1945. Originally, the plans were to build XPBB-1 flying boats at the facility. However, it was later decided that the plant would be used for construction of a large, modern, and as yet undeveloped bomber, the B-29. Since this airplane needed a 5,000-foot runway, one was built adjacent to the plant to the west. Renton eventually constructed 1,119 B-29s with a peak production of six airplanes per day.

ABOVE: The marshland factory site as it looked in September 1941. The lake site was perfect for building and launching flying boats, but only one XPBB-1 was built.

Naturally, when the war ended, almost all orders were cancelled. By 1947 the plant was slated for closure only to be restarted that summer to do modification work. Employment rose to 1,300 with an order for the C-97, a transport version of the B-29.

In 1952 the future of Renton took an entirely new course. The plant was chosen as the site of Boeing's secret new project, the 367-80. The prototype almost immediately demonstrated that it had the qualities to be the world's first truly successful jet airliner. Before long the Air Force ordered a tanker-transport version, the KC-135, of which

The factory immediately after the end of the war with B-29s on the apron in front. From the apron aircraft are towed over the small bridge (lower right) to the airfield.

The first 757 moves into natural light outside the factory at its rollout in 1982. All Boeing's standard-width aircraft are built at Renton and make a similar journey.

806 were built.

With the rollout of the commercial 707 in 1957, 600-miles-per-hour travel became a commonly accepted feature in civilian aviation. Orders from airlines secured positions on an assembly line that has never again seen propellor-driven aircraft.

Boeing, needing more floor space, purchased the plant's 100 acres from the government in 1962. Offices, training facilities, flight lines, manufacturing, electronics, and other activities all needed more space as 707 orders grew. About this time a new smaller airliner was added to the fleet, the 727. Although the 707 was a great success and nearly 1,000 would be built, the 727 would be an even bigger success, and production would eventually exceed that of any previous jet airliner, 1,832 units.

Commercial airplanes grew into Boeing's largest business. Desiring to extend that market, the smaller, short-range 737 was introduced in 1967. Renton, now with three popular airliners coming off the line, was straining the capacity of its site—a victim of its own success. Boeing built a supporting manufacturing facility in Auburn and located plants elsewhere in the Puget Sound area.

Because of the complexity of building airliners, the fast growth in orders was difficult to absorb. Employment in the airplane division tripled between 1964 and 1968. Such growth could not be sustained and was followed by a period of dramatic layoffs in 1970. By 1972, however, business resurgence was obvious and has continued to the present. And by 1982 a new airliner, the 757, was added to the fleet.

Except for a few high-speed hydrofoil boats and militarized 707s, only jetliners have been built in Renton since 1965. Airliners tend to stay in production for many years through constant modernization of the basic design and tailoring each airplane to the requests of the customer airline. With the 5,000th airliner scheduled to roll off its line in 1990, Renton more than any other city has a right to call itself the Jet Capital of the World: Air fleets of the world begin there.

The interior of the Boeing Company factory during B-29 construction. B-29s were too big a project for one factory, and consequently parts came from around North America.

U S WEST COMMUNICATIONS

New Year's Day of 1902 brought more to the City of Renton than just the usual celebration for, on that day, the first telephone exchange was opened at the corner of Third and Main streets. Not too many years before, at the Philadelphia Centennial Exhibition of 1876, Alexander Graham Bell had demonstrated that his newly invented telephone worked but was greeted with skepticism and charges that his invention was merely a gimmick. Bell and his backers obviously disagreed with public opinion, and he created the Bell Telephone Company on July 9, 1877. Slowly, as the practical nature of the telephone became apparent, telephones began to be accepted nationwide.

Renton's citizens, however, followed the skepticism of the rest of the country about the telephone. Even after the town's telephone exchange had been operating for a full year, there were only three telephones in Renton. The exchange's first operator, Bertha Boisseau, who later married James Faull, handled what calls there were on a magneto switchboard, a small cord board with a crank that was used to ring phones.

Business picked up in a hurry, however, for by 1910 two new switchboards of the "C"-frame type were installed. Meanwhile the Bell-owned Sunset Telephone and Telegraph Company had been granted a franchise in 1903 to operate the local telephone firm. But in 1906 a rival had entered the picture: the Renton Telephone and Telegraph Company. In 1912 a separate franchise was granted to the Kent and Renton Telephone and Telegraph Company, which bought out the Sunset firm in April 1914.

The newcomer didn't last long though. The following year Sunset purchased both the Kent and Renton properties, and the entire operation was set up under the operating name of the Pacific Telephone and Telegraph Co., the forerunner of Pacific Northwest Bell.

That same year the telephone was making more momentous—if less confusing news—elsewhere. On January 25, 1915, President Woodrow Wilson made the first transcontinental telephone call from New York to San Francisco. It was a lighthearted if historic occasion for a man who was about to be burdened with the responsibilities of World War I.

There was not only growth in the total number of telephones in Renton but growth in the percentage of its citizens who had them. In 1920 there were 239 telephones to serve 3,000 people; 20 years later 886 phones were in town though the number of people had only increased to 4,026. It was World War II, however, that really changed Renton's telephone needs. The influx of Boeing employees and other defense workers caused Renton to grow quickly from a quiet, small town to a busy population center. Of course, the telephone system had to grow, too.

In May 1942 dial service came to Renton, and new equipment to handle the change was installed in the company's building at 225 Williams Street. Growth following the war continued at a fast clip, and today Renton has 46,000 telephone lines and about 300 employees.

The telecommunications industry continued to change. The Pacific Telephone and Telegraph Company became Pacific Northwest Bell in 1961. On January 1, 1984, the historic divestiture of the Bell System took place. This resulted from changes in technology and a desire to encourage competition in the telecommunications business. On July 1, 1988, the local telephone company's name was changed to U S WEST Communications. What did not change is the commitment to customers, employees, investors, and communities.

Boisseau's Confectionary on Third and Main housed Renton's first telephone exchange. Pictured here is the city's first telephone operator, Bertha Boisseau, who undoubtedly responded with "Hello Central"—the greeting used by telephone operators in towns and cities nationwide. Courtesy, Renton Historical Society

SEATTLE LUMBER COMPANY

The Seattle Lumber Company's larger second building was located at 6797 East Marginal Way in south Seattle, just a short distance from the firm's original site. This building was constructed in the late 1930s.

In 1933, during the Great Depression, Bob Fox and B.L. Lockwood founded Seattle Lumber Company as a local sales organization for lumber exports. At that time the business was located near a mill on East Marginal Way in south Seattle. Later, owing to the expansion of the business, Seattle Lumber moved to 6797 East Marginal Way, just a short distance from its initial site.

Frank Powers, Sr., became a stockholder in 1934, and by 1962, when the company moved to its present Renton location at 500 Southwest 16th Street, the business was wholly owned by Powers. From that time until 1982 Powers ran Seattle Lumber. The senior Powers died in 1983, and Seattle Lumber carries on its tradition of family operation today, with his sons, Frank Jr. and John, as the current heads of the business.

During Seattle Lumber's early years it suffered arson twice. However, the business continued to grow despite these setbacks, and recent years have been free of such occurrences.

Seattle Lumber was the first business to locate in the valley area following the construction of the Howard Hanson Dam to control flooding from the Green River. Indeed, the Powers family bought the property for the Renton business from the heirs of the original homesteaders in the Earlington Flats area. The operation has been located at the same Renton address since the original move from Seattle in 1962, though growth required a major remodeling of the facility in 1984.

Seattle Lumber has always been primarily a lumber distributor, according to Frank Powers, Jr. In the beginning the business revolved around the sale of Douglas fir, but there has been an expansion of the product line over the years, and now kiln-dried lumber, western red cedar, and fire-retardant lumber is available as well. Seattle Lumber also offers associated building materials, hardware, and mill work.

The Seattle area, including Renton, Kent, and Tukwila, is the primary area of distribution for Seattle Lumber. The business employs 10 people, approximately the same number as in the early years.

Seattle Lumber Company and the Powers family have strong ties to Renton. Both Frank Powers, Jr., and John Powers are past presidents of the Greater Renton Chamber of Commerce, and those who work at Seattle Lumber are involved in community-oriented groups.

The Seattle Lumber Company constructed its current building at 500 Southwest 16th Street in Renton in 1962. The building is shown here after extensive remodeling was completed in 1984. Courtesy, Frank Powers, Jr.

RENTON COIL SPRING COMPANY

This is the current site of the Renton Coil Spring Company at 325 Burnett Avenue North in Renton.

When B. Ray Pepka, president of Renton Coil Spring Company, came to visit the Pacific Northwest following World War II, the Indiana resident had no intention of staying or of moving the family business, Pepka Spring Company. Pepka's father and grandfather had worked in the spring-manufacturing business, and Pepka worked for the Kokomo Spring Company from 1930 to 1942 and then for the Pepka Spring Company from 1945 to 1949. Pepka's vacation in the Pacific Northwest so impressed him, however, that he decided to settle in Renton. Within a short time he founded the Renton Coil Spring Company.

The enterprise's first offices were located on Fourth Avenue North, and the business remained in that location for approximately seven years. Then growth in the business necessitated larger quarters, and Renton Coil Spring moved to its second location, on Tobin Street. After another seven prosperous years the plant was moved again, because more space was required, to its current address at 325 Burnett Avenue North.

The springs manufactured today (the spring on the left) are made of titanium and are lighter, stronger, and more corrosion resistant than the old high-carbon steel springs such as the one shown on the right.

The manufacturing of springs has changed a great deal since the early years of the business, according to Charles Pepka, son of Ray Pepka and the general manager of the company. Charles Pepka explains that, until the mid-1960s, a high-carbon steel wire was the material predominately used to make springs. Then stainless-steel and high-temperature alloys were employed. The research developments of the 1980s, in answer to demands for lighter, stronger, and corrosion-resistant springs, dictated that springs be made of titanium, which is the material of choice currently.

Renton Coil Spring has, over the years, manufactured springs for a wide variety of customers. Charles Pepka states that the company's springs have been original equipment on Boeing planes since that firm began making the 707 model. Renton Coil Spring has shared its research with Boeing in order to answer the need for a lighter product. In the 1960s Pepka's company made parts for the moon rover vehicles, and in the 1970s the firm manufactured high-tech springs out of temperature-resistant material for the Westinghouse Company at Hanford, Washington. Pepka explains that commercial space vehicles will be the next important market for his corporation's springs.

Because springs must operate under many kinds of varying conditions, including heat extremes, differing loads, contact with corrosion, and varying velocity stresses, there is a constant need for research in this business. Working with computer-aided design since 1975, when the company became computerized, has helped Renton Coil Spring to respond to the changing requirements of its customers and to continually improve its product. The computer also allows the firm to keep pace with the ongoing research of the aviation industry, which is its primary customer.

Charles Pepka explains that the firm's emphasis on changing with the needs of its customers has allowed Renton Coil Spring Company's 46 employees to improve sales and efficiency. The organization currently sells its product all over the world. In addition, it has been recognized for its effectiveness by receiving the National Small Business Association Award for Excellence in 1978, 1983, and 1984; the award recognizes contributions and service to a nation by a small business.

OLYMPIC PIPE LINE COMPANY

The Renton-based Olympic Pipe Line Company is the major source of refined petroleum products distribution through western Washington, serving the transportation fuel needs of motorists, major airlines, and other energy requirements for residential and commercial comforts.

An underground network of more than 400 miles of pipeline silently and safely meets the ever-increasing demand for these various fuel products. The system originates from petroleum refineries located near the Canadian border, where a 20-inch and a 16-inch pipeline continuously transport the product to major distribution points located in Seattle, Renton, and Sea-Tac Airport. A single 14-inch pipeline continues south from Renton and serves Tacoma, Olympia, Vancouver, and terminates, after crossing under the Columbia River, in Portland, Oregon.

Olympic Pipe Line Company is the major source of refined petroleum products distribution through western Washington. Pictured here is the firm's underground network of more than 400 miles of pipeline. The system originates from petroleum refineries located near the Canadian border.

Pumping stations are strategically located along the pipeline corridor and are designed to boost the flow of product to meet the carefully scheduled consumer demand, which currently exceeds 260,000 barrels of fuel per day.

The focal point of this highly automated pipeline transportation system is the Renton office complex and control center, which is staffed 24 hours per day and maintains the ability to monitor and remotely operate all necessary control functions through a state-of-the-art supervisory system that implements technology to diligently maintain quality control and ensure environmental harmony.

Olympic is very concerned about maintaining the delicate balance between a sound environmental habitat and the demand for gasoline and other fuel products in the Northwest. A great deal of insight was required to provide this compatibility in the inception of the pipeline system, and constant vigilance is maintained to preserve and enhance this relationship.

Though a federally regulated transportation system, Olympic also strives to be a good neighbor to the many municipalities, urban and rural residents, and the host of utilities with which it shares either franchise agreements or easements. An example of this effort can be found in Olympic's public awareness programs, which are designed to inform emergency response agencies and the general public of its location, the nature of the products it transports, and where to direct inquiries for information.

As most of the problems the pipeline encounters are excavation and development of rural properties, Olympic also belongs to, and is a resounding advocate of, the Underground Utility Notification Center. Any excavator is required to notify the center, which in turn notifies the utility for marking or identification prior to the excavation. Olympic receives and responds to approximately 75 messages daily

Olympic Pipe Line Company employs more than 60 full-time personnel, who are responsible for the operation of the system. Additional construction and maintenance firms are contracted as necessary, thereby contributing to the local economy and maintaining a strong bond with the City of Renton. Having served the Northwest for 25 years, and realizing the future energy needs, Olympic will strive to maintain both its quality of product and its niche in a delicate environment, thereby assuring present and future residents of its long-term commitment.

The Renton office complex and control center of Olympic Pipe Line Company is staffed 24 hours per day and maintains the ability to monitor and remotely operate all neccessary control functions through a state-of-the-art supervisory system.

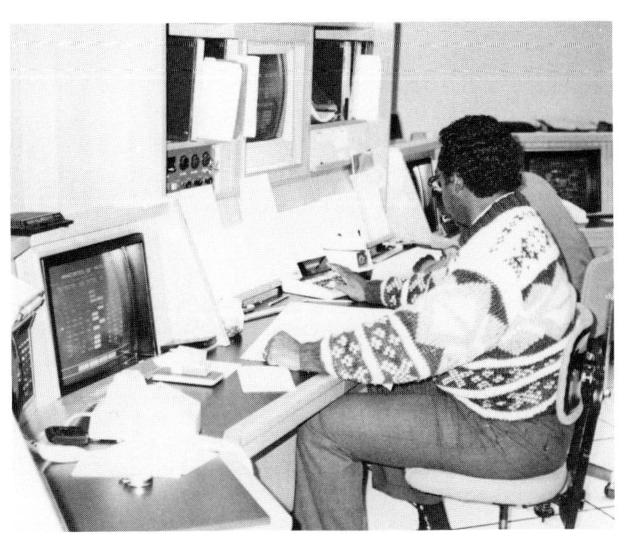

TONKIN FAMILY RESTAURANTS

Frank Tonkin has lived in Renton all of his life. His family has been in Renton since his grandfather, James Tonkin, settled there in 1884 and started Tonkin's General Store, located on the corner of Houser Way and Williams Street. The store, which was a family-operated business, moved in 1915 to the corner of Third and Williams streets. Frank Tonkin, along with his brothers, Wes, Harold, and Bud, worked in the store as young men.

Though Frank has a great deal of business experience prior to the 1933 opening of Tonkin's Cafe (and Turf), it was then that his career as a restaurateur really began. Tonkin did everything in the operation of his family business, including preparation, cooking, waiting on customers, acting as busboy, and washing dishes. With its convenient location, Tonkin's Cafe (and Turf) became a landmark and was noted for its quality food such as pot pies, Swiss steak, and homemade desserts. The cafe was so successful that in 1939 the business moved down Third Street between Wells and Williams because more room was required to accommodate customer demand. At this time, and for several years, Tonkin's was one of *the* restaurants in Renton. The larger site was expanded in 1955 with an addition as still more space was needed. Wes Tonkin operated the Toggery, a men's clothing store, next door to the cafe.

Tonkin's Cafe was one of Frank Tonkin's early (1933) and successful restaurant ventures. Pictured here is the cafe in its original location in the Tonkin Building.

Though the firm was very much a family business, a long-lasting business relationship was formed with Iola Nelson, a C.P.A. who became the accountant for the business. She has remained with the Tonkins over the past 40 years.

When Frank Tonkin sold the cafe in 1965, he did not retire. He continued to operate Bif's, which he had opened in 1958. This successful fast-food hamburger restaurant was located on the corner of Second Street and Rainier Avenue. Because of his experience with Bif's, Frank Tonkin's interest in the fast-food industry was well established when he learned of the Taco Time concept. His interest in a Mexican fast-food outlet had been piqued by a friend who had told him that a place featuring that concept had opened a few months earlier in Tacoma. He believed that people's desire for fresh, good-tasting food would not be hampered by an unfamiliar menu. Eventually, in 1971, Bif's became a Taco Time.

When Frank Tonkin opened his first Taco Time restaurant in 1962, Taco Time was a franchised company based in Eugene, Oregon. Though the parent company is still located there, in 1979 western Washington became an independent operation with Tonkin incorporating Accord, Inc., as the franchisor for the region. Today the three Taco Time restaurants in Renton are all operated by the Tonkin family.

Frank Tonkin, along with his son Jim, proceeded with his venture and opened another Taco Time in Alki in 1963. The fresh sauces, vegetables, and meats, which were, and still are, prepared daily, helped to ensure the popularity of the Taco Time concept.

An artist's rendering of the New Taco Time office that will be built in 1989. The new offices will be located one mile east of I-405 on the Maple Valley Highway in Renton.

The restaurants flourished. There was amazing growth in the business in the 1970s, and that growth continues today, with 68 stores currently operating in western Washington and another five planned for opening in 1989.

At first the Taco Time Restaurant had a limited menu with only crisp tacos and crisp burritos offered. The Mexican menu has been expanded considerably over the years, and currently a variety of choices, including salads and desserts, are available.

There have been other significant changes in the company since its inception. At first the restaurants were little more than roadside stands, with little or no seating. They are now comfortably appointed with spacious dining areas. In addition, the introduction of the drive-through window in the 1970s has changed the business. More customers drop by for snacks or for a quick meal while they are on the road.

Another important way in which Taco Time has changed is in the size in its staff. Taco Time in Renton started with 15 employees who were mostly Tonkin family members. It currently employs more than 500 people in the area. Taco Time has more than 1,300 employees throughout western Washington.

Jim Tonkin is president of Accord, Inc., the franchisor for Taco Time's western Washington operations. Jim's sons, Bob and Matt, along with their responsibilities in directing operations of 21 restaurants, are also involved in purchasing, product development, site selection, and construction.

In keeping with their family-operated restaurant tradition, the Tonkin clan is once more venturing forth with a new concept. Scheduled to open in the fall of 1989 in the South Center Food Court is a specialty chicken restaurant serving prepared fresh daily chicken sandwiches, pot pies, soups, salads, corn bread, and gourmet fried chicken under the logo of U.S. Chicken.

The Accord, Inc., offices, which are currently located next to the Carco Theatre Park and the community center, will be replaced by new offices, housed in a two-story, 8,000-square-foot building. The structure will also have a 4,000-square-foot warehouse. These facilities will be located just one mile east of the present offices.

Taco Time's involvement with the community over the years has kept pace with the firm's growth. For years Taco Time has sponsored local Little League teams. With the introduction of the Renton River Days Festival, Taco Time has sponsored the Renton All-City Band, which is made up of student musicians throughout the area. The Taco Time restaurants have also been involved with the local chapter of the American Cancer Society and in many special events held by schools and community groups. These activities reflect the concern of the Tonkins for the community in which they had their beginnings—and where they plan a thriving future.

The First Taco Time restaurant that Frank Tonkin opened was in White Center in 1962.

HOLMES ELECTRIC COMPANY

Holmes Electric Company was founded on January 1, 1946, by J.E. Holmes and Eugene M. Richards; it has been a closely knit, family-run operation ever since. With the two founders as the only employees and Holmes' wife, Karmen, as the secretary and bookkeeper, the company opened for business, operating at 237 Garden Avenue. The firm grew quickly; in 1947 it was moved to larger quarters at 331 Main Street. Fired in part by the postwar building boom, the expanding business required still larger accommodations and was moved again in 1949 to the corner of Third and Cedar in Renton. There it remained until 1969, when another site was chosen at 1415 Seneca. The company moved to its present location at 1422 Raymond in 1980.

In Holmes Electric's early days it was well known in Renton by its popular slogan, "Holmes Wires Homes." In addition, the firm had a large reader board at the Third and Cedar location that posted various sayings from "Old Man Holmes." An example of one message posted on this board was, "Do you want a better job—done faster, costing less? Let 'my boys' be your electrician." The reader board messages became sort of a landmark in Renton, and it became a point of interest to see what would be posted on it next. In the early days of the company there were many promotional projects, such as floats for the Longacres Day celebration, participation in the Renton Exposition in the late 1940s, and the establishment, in 1947, of an appliance division, which continued until 1969.

Though the company made its reputation as primarily a residential wiring contractor, Holmes Electric began doing commercial wiring exclusively in 1969, and electrical contracting has become its primary business. Some of the many businesses that Holmes Electric has served are Longacres; Boeing; 2 Union Square, a 55-story office building in Seattle; and numerous others.

This is the first office site of Holmes Electric Company at 237 Garden Avenue in Renton.

From its inception Holmes Electric Company has had an active and accessible service department that currently has a fleet of 30 trucks that are on call 24 hours per day for emergency service. The service department responds to requests from both residential and commercial customers.

Holmes Electric Company has been a family business from the start and continues that tradition today. Though founder J.E. Holmes died in 1982, his son, Jeray A. Holmes, continues as president of the firm, a position he has held since 1985. Richards, the company's co-founder, is the executive vice-president, while his son, Michael W. Richards, went to work for the organization in 1972 and presently is its secretary/treasurer. The strong family ties of the business continue into the third generation with Michael Holmes, son of Jeray and Carolyn Holmes, joining the company in 1984 as vice-president.

According to Eugene Richards and Michael Holmes, the firm is keeping pace with the changing technology by expanding its offerings into fiber optics, data cabling, and telephone cabling. Though Holmes Electric Company will retain electrical contracting as its primary business, it has sought to respond to the special needs of its technology-based customers.

After several changes of address, each move made to accommodate the firm's growth, Holmes Electric Company moved into its present modern headquarters at 1422 Raymond in 1980.

A&H STORES, INC.

On May 4, 1946, Johnny Austin and Robert Hendrickson, both pharmacists, founded the Austin-Hendrickson Pharmacy at 301 Third Avenue in Renton. The business was, at first, largely operated by family members. Austin and Hendrickson were the pharmacists. Their wives, June and Jeanellen, helped fixture the store and merchandise the shelves. Jean Hendrickson continued to clerk and still works part time in the Renton store.

Johnny Austin (left) and Robert Hendrickson, co-founders of A&H Stores, are shown behind the counter of their first store at 301 Third Avenue in Renton in the late 1940s.

The business that began operating in a 1,500-square-foot store expanded to a second location with the opening of another store in the Renton Highlands in 1958. Additional stores soon followed, with locations in Kent, Auburn, and Skyway, so that the entire Renton area had A&H drugstores. The series of partnerships was incorporated in 1968.

Though four of the five original stores initially had soda fountains, it was not a trend that was to continue; the rising costs of operating the fountains could not be offset by increasing prices. "Many people would enjoy a cup of coffee for five cents, and our limited menu of lunches and ice cream could not support the floor space devoted to food," explains Hendrickson. According to Hendrickson, specialty ice cream stores, which could offer a wide selection of flavors, and the growing popularity of fast-food restaurants combined to make the drugstore fountains a piece of Americana whose time was past.

Currently there are nine A&H drugstores and 13 card shops throughout the area from Bellingham to Tacoma. Approximately 200 people are employed by the company.

Though Austin passed away in July 1989, Hendrickson continues as chairman of the board. Two of the Hendrickson sons are now involved—Richard is the president of A&H; Stacey is its general counsel. The other Hendrickson children Janine, a teacher, and Scott, a psychologist, are not involved in A&H Stores, Inc.

Hendrickson explains that there have been many changes in the drugstore business over the years. The field has become very competitive with the advent of large chain drugstores, discount stores, and the "one-stop" grocery store/drugstore combinations. The "bigger the better" concept has resulted in many of the independent drugstore owners getting out of the business. An example of this can be seen when one realizes that downtown Renton once had five drugstores, but only two remain after all the changes in the business.

He sees their future growth of the business as being in the direction of a "professional store" that fills prescriptions exclusively and is conveniently located near clinics. He further explains that since the advent of second-party payees, usually the individual's medical insurance, price competition is almost eliminated. Thus, in order to succeed, pharmacies must rely on their other strengths—efficient service, convenient location, and the confidence that can be built between the customer and the family pharmacist.

Despite foreseeing continued changes in the health care system, Hendrickson says, "Pharmacies won't be phased out; there will always be a need to fill prescriptions."

Pictured is one of the many A&H stores that currently stretch from Bellingham to Tacoma.

FIRST FEDERAL SAVINGS AND LOAN ASSOCIATION OF RENTON

Conservative management and continuity have produced a high level of depositor trust in First Federal Savings and Loan Association of Renton, according to the man who has been the president of that institution since 1961, Harry A. Blencoe. Since beginning his banking career at First Federal as a new graduate of the University of Washington in 1950, Blencoe has served First Federal in several capacities, including assistant secretary in 1951, executive vice-president in 1957, a board member since 1959, and president since 1961. Blencoe has been the president of First Federal longer than any other individual, and during his tenure, he has seen the assets of the organization grow from less than $3.6 million to almost $192.46 million as of June 30, 1988, with a net worth of roughly $14.3 million. Such growth becomes even more impressive when First Federal's unique position among savings institutions is realized; it has no borrowed money and is rated one of the financially strongest thrifts in the nation.

Prior to Blencoe's years as an employee and president, First Federal Savings and Loan's roots were deep in the Renton community. In 1923 E.C. Wilson founded the institution, which was incorporated under the name of the Renton Savings and Loan Association. It was an offshoot of the Wilson & Marlowe real estate firm, which had been representing a Seattle savings institution by taking real estate loan applications and accepting deposits.

E.P. Wilson, son of the founder, took over in 1935 following the death of his father, and on April 25, 1935, the name was changed to First Federal Savings and Loan Association of Renton. It then became a federally chartered association. That year was especially significant for First Federal because on May 6, 1935, the institution was accepted for insurance of savings accounts by the Federal Savings and Loan Insurance Corporation, which then insured savings up to $5,000 per account.

E.P. Wilson left First Federal Savings in 1941, and R.E. Theinhardt became the institution's president in June of that year. At this time the institution was reorganized, and a new board of directors was named. The new directors were Theinhardt, John Swanson, Hayden Williams, Alec Pelto, Warren Williams, Charles Flash, and Floyd Lawrence. Growth continued for First Federal Savings during the 1940s, with assets increasing from $910,663 at the end of 1941 to roughly $2.87 million by the close of 1945 and growing to exceed $3.5 million by the time Blencoe began his career at First Federal in 1950.

The strength of First Federal

ABOVE: First Federal Savings and Loan has been at its present location on the corner of Second Street and Wells Avenue since 1967, though an addition was made in 1979.

Harry A. Blencoe, longtime president of First Federal Savings and Loan Association of Renton, enters that institution's offices to begin another day's work.

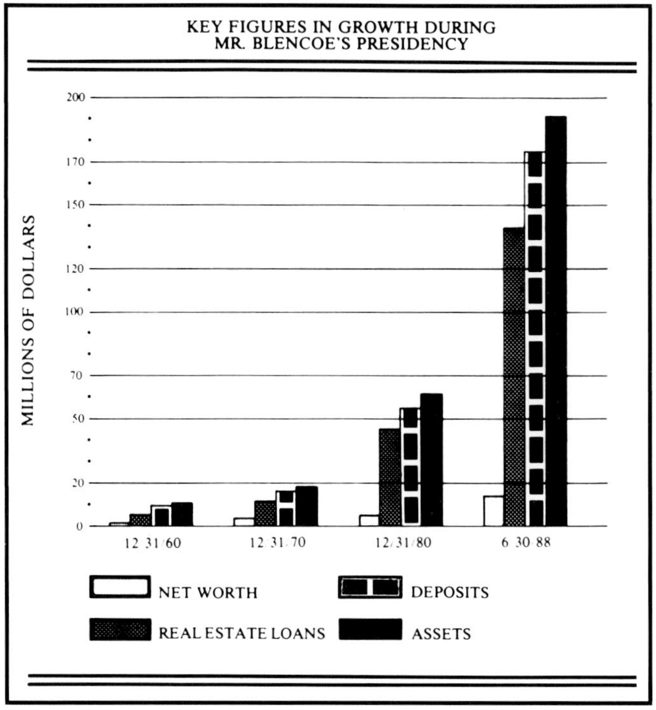

Savings has continued, according to Blencoe, in large part owing to the solid reputation of the institution coupled with ongoing emphasis on treating employees, customers, and officers fairly and courteously. The resulting loyalty, Blencoe states, is evident in the statistic that First Federal Savings has a larger percentage of all deposits in Renton, even though there are 26 other financial institutions within five miles.

First Federal Savings of Renton, the home office, attracts customers from all parts of the area and even out of state. First Federal Savings has depositors who live in Sweden, Australia, Japan, England, and the Philippines, to name a few.

States Blencoe, "Word of mouth advertising has been our best marketing tool at First Federal. One satisfied customer tells another—the word gets around. Everyone in the banking business knows about our conservative management and credibility."

The stability of First Federal Savings can be seen even in its location. The offices were moved four times in the early years of the institution, when larger quarters were required. The current location of First Federal Savings has been the same since the building was constructed in early 1967 on the corner of Second Street and Wells Avenue South. An addition to the present building was made in 1979. Currently there are no branch offices of First Federal Savings, though Blencoe does not rule out that possibility in the future. First Federal has stayed with one central location because, as Blencoe states, "customers will find a strong institution."

The unity at First Federal Savings is further strengthened by the harmonious working atmosphere and the longevity of its staff. First Federal Savings currently employs 26 people, and several of those employees have been with the firm for more than 22 years. The turnover rate is so low that there have been six people who have retired from First Federal Savings after years of service. Blencoe states that sensitivity in management is largely responsible for such a stable group of employees, and he strives to keep negative feelings out of the work place. "I want my employees to feel good about themselves," states Blencoe.

First Federal officers and employees are continuously seeking new ideas to improve the many services for their customers. Both officers and employees are encouraged to attend classes and seminars to update their skills and knowledge of the savings and loan business. At First Federal the employees are quick to show or demonstrate the latest equipment; in fact, it has been said on many occasions that First Federal has many procedures and programs that one would only expect from a much larger financial institution.

The members of the board of directors of First Federal Savings and Loan Association of Renton take special pride in trying to encourage management to be up to date in every respect in offering the latest competitive services at the fairest price possible. The current members of the board are Dr. Gary F. Kohlwes, Andrew Gigli, Robert L. Anderson, Gerald Edlund, Robert McLendon, and H.A. Blencoe.

During his tenure, Harry A. Blencoe has seen the assets of First Federal grow from less than $3.6 million to almost $192.46 million as of June 30, 1988, with a net worth of roughly $14.3 million.

GROUP HEALTH COOPERATIVE

Today the cooperative has a membership of 400,000 throughout Washington, and the Renton Center's membership has swelled to 23,000.

The Renton Medical Center of the Group Health Cooperative was founded in 1949, just one year after the Group Health Cooperative had acquired its hospital on 15th Avenue and East John Street in Seattle. The Renton Center had the same philosophy as its parent organization—providing a program of health promotion and preventative care as well as services for those who were ill. Since the people of Renton needed local health care at a reasonable price, a handful of citizens got together and began the first clinic, housed in a little brick building on Third Street. An optometrist and an obstetrician/gynecologist shared the same office when the clinic opened its doors.

Since the early days, when the entire Group Health Cooperative had only 140,000 members, there has been considerable growth. Today the cooperative has a membership of 400,000 throughout Washington, and the Renton Center's membership has swelled to 23,000. Members participate in an annual prepaid plan that has no deductibles. Each member chooses his or her own doctor, and all of the staff is salaried.

In 1968 the Renton Center's current facilities at 275 Bronson Way Northeast were built with Hill-Burton funds. The center has continued to expand its services so that it now has 13 family practice specialists, 3 pediatricians, 2 physicians' assistants, 2 optometrists, and a pediatric nurse practitioner who is master's prepared and sees her own practice. In the same building several ancillary services are offered, including a pharmacy, lab, X-ray facilities, physical therapy, speech and hearing, and a "see center" for prescriptions for glasses.

According to Sharen Stoll, who is the clinic administrator and a registered nurse with a master's degree in business administration, in addition to these services Group Health is responsible for a number of innovations in the health care field. The company began a consulting nurse program 15 years ago in which patients can call and talk with highly trained nurses. A record of the call is placed in the patient's file. The Renton Center has four consulting nurses, who, on a rotating basis, respond to patients' questions over the telephone. In addition, the Renton Center has several specialty nurses, such as a triage nurse who does assessment of a patient's needs, an injection room nurse, and two pediatric nurses who specialize in well-baby care. There are also a head nurse and a nursing director in management positions.

Staff at the Renton facility includes one licensed assistant for each physician and a medical receptionist for every two to three physicians.

A staff of 120 employees at the Renton Center, who have been with the center an average of 15 years, see 70,000 people annually. The staff is encouraged to participate in continuing education programs and, according to Stoll, Group Health has more board-certified staff members than most, if not all, other health care facilities in the Seattle area.

True to its philosophy of health promotion, the Renton Center offers a variety of courses for members on a rotating basis. The courses vary widely according to member interests, and many are self-supporting, while others require a small fee.

Located at 275 Bronson Way Northeast, the Renton Center of Group Health Cooperative provides a program of health promotion and preventative care as well as services for those who are ill.

BARBEE MILL

On November 29, 1929, Jim Carlson and James Weter founded the Seattle-Renton Mill on the site where the Renton Municipal Airport now stands. When the mill began operations, the average production was 50,000 board feet per day with 40 men to the shift. In addition to the lumber produced, there were many by-products that also found a market. The sawdust was sold as an inexpensive fuel for home use, and the scraps were pulverized and used to fire larger boilers.

George Bush made a campaign stop at Barbee Mill during the 1988 presidential campaign.

Things changed for the Seattle-Renton Mill with the advent of World War II. The government purchased the mill and hired Mr. Barbee, a ship and barge builder in Ballard, to run the mill as a construction plant for the barges needed in the war effort.

In 1943 the government decided to sell the mill to Barbee and use the site for construction of the Renton Airfield. Barbee located a suitable place for mill operations across Lake Washington near Kennydale, disassembled the plant, and towed all of the equipment across the lake on barges to the mill's present site. The company became Barbee Mill and manufactured barges and tugs until the war's conclusion.

In 1945 Barbee sold the mill to Alex Cugini, Sr., and his wife, Josephine, who used the mill to produce lumber. Their son, Alex Cugini, Jr., joined the family business in 1950 as the mill manager. At that time there were 13 sawmills operating in the greater Seattle area, today only Barbee Mill remains.

Alex Cugini, Jr., explains that both the competitive nature of the sawmill industry and the shrinking timber supply are primary reasons for the dwindling number of mills. Barbee Mill, however, is a strong business that operates 20 hours per day with two shifts of workers and directly employs 125 people. The automated mill produces 125,000 feet of board measure per shift, much of which is metric-size lumber destined for foreign markets, especially Japan. More than 90 percent of the lumber produced at the mill is sold abroad.

Barbee Mill has had its share of difficulties. In 1957 a fire started by children playing with matches totally destroyed the mill. The loss exceeded one million dollars; but that did not stop the Cugini family, who completely rebuilt the entire operation by 1959.

Alex Cugini, Sr., continued as the head of the business until his death in 1978, when his wife and son, Alex, Jr., took over the leadership of Barbee Mill. The tradition of a family-operated business continues, with Alex Jr. as president, Josephine as a vice-president and treasurer, daughter Catherine as secretary, and son Robert as a vice-president.

According to Alex Cugini, Jr., the future of Barbee Mill depends on such variables as exchange rates and the availability of raw material. The company continues to seek new markets, he states; shipments to Australia and Europe are examples of this effort. The firm has diversified, and for the past 15 years the Barbee International Company has existed not only for the sale of timber, but also products such as wine and fish. He also credits mill automation with new sawing techniques and size control, which produces far less waste and increases overall efficiency as well as output.

An aerial view of Barbee Mill, located on the shores of Lake Washington. The mill produces 125,000 feet of board measure per shift, much of which is metric-size lumber destined for foreign markets, especially Japan.

VALLEY MEDICAL CENTER

World War II, which brought so many changes to Renton, affected yet another vital area of the community—its hospital system. Prior to the war the small town of Renton had been served by Bronson Hospital. The massive number of defense workers that flooded Renton during the war, coupled with the limited capacity of Bronson Hospital, dictated that new hospital facilities be quickly and substantially increased.

In 1942 the City of Renton got approval from the Public Buildings Administration to begin constructing a 100-bed facility on Rainier Avenue. When the hospital was completed in 1944, it was discovered that Renton did not have the power to operate hospitals, thus the new facility could not open. Efforts to find another governmental body to run the hospital were unsuccessful. It was not until nine citizens formed Valley Foundation, Inc., to lease the facility that the Renton Hospital was able to open its doors on April 15, 1945.

Valley Medical Center has grown from the 100-bed Renton Hospital into a 303-bed comprehensive care facility.

Following the war the state legislature passed a law in 1947 that allowed voters to create a taxing district for the ownership and operation of hospitals. In the general election of 1948, such a district was approved by the voters along with a bond issue for the purchase of the Renton Hospital from the federal government. On January 5, 1948, the first public hospital district in the state, District No. 1 of King County, was formed, and the hospital was purchased for $200,000.

On January 5, 1948, public hospital district No. 1 of King County was formed, and the Renton Hospital was purchased from the federal government.

By 1965 Renton Hospital had become inadequate to serve the needs of the area, and, since it had been built 20 years earlier as a temporary facility, there were many problems with the physical plant. Planning began for the construction of a new building. At that time an area contest was held to find a name that reflected the hospital's actual service to the community, and so Renton Hospital became Valley General Hospital. In November 1966 the voters approved a $7-million bond issue for the construction of a new hospital at 400 South 43rd Street, and the hospital doors opened in November 1969 with a 254-bed capacity.

Since Valley General opened, there have been several expansions: In 1977 additional special treatment centers and 49 beds were added, and a 1983 growth spurt brought the total licensed bed capacity to 303. In 1984 the Radiation-Oncology Unit was opened, and the name of the hospital was changed to Valley Medical Center to reflect the comprehensive care offered. Recent expansion includes completion of a 100,000-square-foot medical office building and a 300-stall parking garage, and a 1990 opening of a 40-bed general and medical psychiatric unit is planned.

Throughout the history of Valley Medical Center there have only been four administrators: Charlotte Dowler, 1944 to 1949; M.C. Lund, 1949 to 1965; William E. Murray, 1966 to 1983; and Richard Roodman, 1983 to the present.

In addition to the health care available at Valley Medical, the hospital also tries to fulfill its goal of being responsive to patients and the community by offering a number of related health promotion classes and services to the area. One innovative program available is Valley Medical's GoldenCare Plus. This free service offers senior citizens assistance with medical bill questions and provides members with information about programs available at Valley Medical Center.

With these facilities and services, Valley Medical Center seeks to fulfill its mission: "to assure that the health care needs of people living in its principal service area are met" by promoting "high-quality care, appropriate use of resources, and cost-effective delivery of services."

WASHINGTON NATURAL GAS

When the first gaslights lit the way through the streets of Renton in 1912, they were beacons for a new wave of modernization in the city.

It was not long before advertisements in the *Renton Herald* boasted about the modern gas ranges that provided a "clean, comfortable kitchen to cook in" with a "labor-, time-, and money-saving range to cook on." The Cottage Arc gaslight was proclaimed the light that "gives the greatest illumination of any light ever made at a cost of about one-third of a cent per hour. It can be lighted or extinguished simply by pulling the chain."

Renton citizens also were learning that gas heaters had qualities that would inexpensively enhance the comfort of their homes. In another *Renton Herald* advertisement, the gas company asked, "Ever use a gas heater? Just the thing for that cold bedroom or bathroom, priced from $1.50 up."

Adding to the modernization of twentieth-century homes, other products, including gas water heaters, gas griddles, and gas irons, joined the line of gas appliances on the market.

In 1956 natural gas replaced manufactured gas. Natural gas flowed into the state through major new pipelines linking Puget Sound customers with gas fields in the American Southwest and Canada. Just one year prior to that, the Seattle Gas Company, serving Seattle, Renton, Kent, and Tukwila, merged with Washington Gas and Electric in Tacoma to form Washington Natural Gas.

This 1912 advertisement in the *Renton Herald* invites residents to watch gas cooking demonstrations on a modern gas range.

Because natural gas is one of the most easily controlled sources of energy, local industries saw natural gas as a benefit to their business. Industries throughout the area use gas for everything from firing furnaces and kilns to forging, cutting, hardening, drying, purifying, fabricating, processing, curing, and shaping materials.

In 1964 Washington Natural Gas invited Renton citizens to an open house for its new office on Third Avenue. The new facility featured a display of the latest gas appliances and home heating equipment. The Blue Flame Room, designed for home service demonstrations and seating approximately 30 people, was available for use by private organizations. The office provided convenient service to approximately 8,000 customers in the rapidly growing Renton-Kent-Tukwila area.

Today the Renton office, still located at the same address on Third Avenue, serves customers in Renton, Kent, Tukwila, and surrounding areas. As in 1964 the area continues to grow. Employees in the Renton office are active in community events such as the Renton River Days, a celebration held every summer. Washington Natural Gas provides a hot water tank for dish washing during the event.

Washington Natural Gas is a subsidiary of Washington Energy Company, which has operations in 13 states and three Canadian provinces. The parent company's interests include distribution of natural gas, marketing of energy, conservation services and products, coal holdings, and oil and gas exploration and development. Washington Natural Gas serves more than 326,000 residential, commercial, and industrial customers in five counties—Snohomish, Thurston, Pierce, King, and Lewis. The company provides more energy each year than any other utility in the state.

A vintage photograph of a gas company sales floor, with a display of gas heating equipment.

S. JOHN VUKOV, M.D.

When Dr. S.J. Vukov opened his medical practice in the Wood's building on Third Avenue and Main Street in Renton, office calls were three dollars, and housecalls were five dollars. Renton had 3,670 residents, and the year was 1940. Until his retirement in 1987, Dr. Vukov played a vital role, literally, in the growth of Renton. He estimates that during his 47 years of practice he delivered 9,500 babies, almost double the town's 1940 population. Throughout his long practice the stories of his readiness in any emergency, his compassionate manner, and, when the situation warranted, his toughness spread, making him a legendary figure.

After World War I young Vukov (age 12), his older brother, and his mother traveled from the Island of Zlarin on Yugoslavia's Adriatic Coast to Seattle, where his father was already established as a member of the large Dalmation fishing community. Dr. Vukov himself worked 13 summers on commercial salmon vessels to sustain his studies. He was educated first at a Seattle high school, where he completed his studies in 2.5 years, then at the University of Washington, where he received a bachelor's degree in Pharmacy. He then went on to the University of Oregon for his medical degree.

The young Dr. Vukov then went for additional training at Harborview Hospital in Seattle. There, during the last years of the Depression, he encountered a wide variety of cases, since masses of poor people of that era could not get medical care anywhere else. Dr. Vukov's work began to receive some recognition when, in 1939, he treated a young man who had Type 12 pneumococcus meningitis and cured him. This feat was widely noted as the first recorded cure of this disease, and articles were written about it. Dr. Vukov later presented the young man at a conference of physicians to show that the boy had been cured without after effects. That same year the doctor published an article about his work using Vitamin K as an aid to blood clotting. This article prompted worldwide inquiries. Both articles were published in the *Northwest Medical Journal*.

The stuff of legends—for a half-century, Dr. Vukov treated patients like family.

Dr. Vukov's growing reputation proved helpful in another way in addition to the professional recognition it gave him. He was offered a job working mornings at the University of Washington Health Center. Trying to make ends meet, he took yet another position; he became the doctor for the members of the Eagles lodge in Renton. The guaranteed 10 cents per person per month for taking care of the lodge members and their families helped financially

A dramatic head-on collision between two trains in downtown Renton on July 4, 1955, helped build Dr. John Vukov's reputation as the man to call on in an emergency. Vukov, shown here standing on the ladder, eventually had to amputate the leg of a trapped engineer in order to free him.

through the first two years of his practice. He also worked as a contract surgeon at Ft. Lewis. Everything changed two years later.

Prior to his entry into the U.S. Army in 1942, he and three other young physicians—Deane Pettibone, M.D.; Milton Schultz, M.D.; and John Carney, M.D.—lobbied the government to work on the military industrial complex being built in the Renton area. The small and aging Bronson Hospital was deemed antiquated and inadequate for the area. They were successful, and after 4.5 years of military service they returned to their new Renton hospital, which opened in April 1945.

Dr. Vukov recalls those days as unbelievably harried. Though he was a general surgeon, the rapid population growth, the few physicians, and Renton Hospital's status as the only facility in south King County meant that he did a bit of everything. He performed a multitude of types of surgery, from ingrown toenails and complex bone repair to extensive abdominal surgery. He, at times, even had to perform emergency brain surgery when there was only one neurosurgeon in the greater Seattle area.

Drawing from his wide experiences over the years, he recalls some especially memorable cases. One of the most dramatic emergencies happened on July 4, 1955, at noon, when two trains collided head on in downtown Renton. The doctor, who had been gardening when he received the call to "come right away," had no idea what had happened until he arrived. What he saw was a mass of twisted wreckage, one dead engineer, and the other engineer, John Severson, Jr., clinging to life but trapped. Dr. Vukov and the others worked to free him, but could not release the man's pinned leg. Finally the doctor set up an operating theater on the engine and amputated Severson's leg at the thigh. The incident brought Vukov much recognition, and the pictures of the accident appeared on the front page of the *New York Times* and on national television.

Dr. Vukov's practice grew, and in 1959 he built the clinic at Second Street and Park Avenue that bears his name today, though it is now run by other physicians.

Not all battles were at the bedside or accident scene. In addition to his many other contributions to the Renton community, he was instrumental in securing a permanent hospital for the area. In the late 1940s the government decided to sell the Renton Hospital, and Group Health wanted to purchase it. Dr. Vukov was concerned that physicians would then have to send their patients to Seattle, and he began trying to solve the problem. He, together with Earl Maxwell, then a state senator from Renton, the Greater Renton Chamber of Commerce, civic leaders, and other doctors, approached the state legislature.

Dr. John Vukov, seen here standing in front of the Vukov Clinic, built the facility, which is located at Second Street and Park Avenue, in Renton in 1959. The structure still bears his name, although he has retired from the practice of medicine.

Maxwell created a plan for raising building funds by establishing a hospital district, and a bill was put together, the first of its kind in the state. This was a new concept—to create such a district there, as well as anywhere in the United States. After much arduous lobbying, the bill passed at the last moment of the last day of the legislative session. This allowed for the future facility, known as Valley Medical Center, to be built. The city and the area owe a great deal to Senator Earl Maxwell.

Since his retirement at age 75, Dr. Vukov has continued with his active life. He swims daily, attends seminars at various institutions of learning, hunts, fishes, and travels with his wife. Looking back on his long career, he believes that the fact that he lived and learned through the Depression made a profound impression on him. It showed him the great value of life and the need to alleviate human suffering. He describes himself as a dedicated physician—dedicated to his patients. He says that he always "treated people first and collected later" if he could and asserts, "I never denied anyone treatment because he couldn't pay."

PACCAR INC

Founded by William Pigott, the Seattle Car Manufacturing Company began its operations in 1905 as a small firm located in West Seattle. There the company produced railcars to transport logs for Washington's growing timber industry. By the end of its first year, the fledgling enterprise became quite successful, and plant operations were expanded. The firm's product line also grew, and soon Seattle Car, which would later become PACCAR Inc, was making many different types of railcars.

With increasing needs for even larger facilities, Seattle Car relocated in 1908 to a new plant site in Renton. Three years later the company changed its name to Seattle Car & Foundry Company. By 1917 Seattle Car merged with Twohy Brothers Company of Portland, another leading Northwest railcar manufacturer, to form the Pacific Car & Foundry Company. The new firm, with plants in both Renton and Portland, achieved immediate success with a government order for 2,000 boxcars needed to transport freight during World War I.

In 1924 Pigott sold Pacific Car to pursue other interests in the steel business. Under new ownership, the company diversified into manufacturing buses, structural-steel fabrications, and metal technology. Motivated by deep pride in the company's history and the promise of diversifying into new product areas, Paul Pigott, William's son, repurchased Pacific Car in 1934.

During World War II Pacific Car built more than 900 Sherman tanks and wing spars for American bombers. The Renton plant also produced nearly 1,400 tank recovery vehicles for the war effort.

With the close of World War II, as the peacetime market for trucks increased, Pacific Car acquired Kenworth Truck Company. During this time the firm also found itself to be a leading manufacturer of railcars as the demand for this product grew. The year 1953 proved to be an important one for the company: It began to produce mechanical refrigeration cars, which did not require the use of salt that had proved so corrosive to car frames in the past. Holding below-zero temperatures for long periods of time, these cars were also an improvement over the old ice-cooled variety in terms of weight and volume. It was not long before Pacific Car became the industry leader in the production of refrigeration cars.

After the close of World War II, Pacific Car found that the railcar market was booming. Refrigerator cars, such as these, became so important to the company, that, by 1953, Pacific Car was the leading builder of refrigerator and insulated cars.

Pacific Car's diversification progressed with continuing military contracts, the acquisition in 1958 of the Dart Truck Company, and the purchase of Peterbilt Motors Company, a heavy-duty truck manufacturer.

In 1965 Charles M. Pigott, Paul's son, was elected president of Pacific Car & Foundry. Four years later, still growing rapidly, the firm moved its corporate headquarters to Bellevue. In 1972 the company was consolidated and renamed PACCAR Inc. However, the Pacific Car & Foundry name was retained for the foundry and manufacturing operations for winches and railcars at the Renton plant.

For the next several years success continued. When Renton celebrated its

The Seattle Car Manufacturing Company which later became PACCAR Inc, was one of the first U.S. companies to make and sell rail passenger cars to China in 1908.

Diamond Jubilee in 1976, Pacific Car was the second-largest employer in town. In 1980 employment figures at the Renton plant peaked at more than 2,000. However, when the railcar market came to a halt, PACCAR formed PACCAR Defense Systems in the mid-1980s—a new division created to procure government defense contracts. In 1988 PACCAR refocused its government business and relocated the operation to Kirkland. During this time the Renton manufacturing facility was phased out.

Diversification has long been one of the hallmarks of PACCAR, and since it first sold railcars to China in 1908, the company has sought to grow with the marketplace. During the 1980s PACCAR acquired Foden Trucks and Trico Industries, Inc.—an oil pumping and extraction equipment company. PACCAR also diversified into the general automotive parts and accessories market through its acquisition of more than 130 Grand Auto and Al's Auto Supply stores located in California, Nevada, Washington, and Alaska. In yet another product area, the firm produces the world's most extensive line of trackless vehicles for underground mining and tunneling through its Wagner Mining Equipment Co.

With sales in 1988 of $3.1 billion, PACCAR employs approximately 14,000 people worldwide. PACCAR maintains exceptionally high standards of quality for its products, which are well engineered, highly customized for particular applications, and priced to sell in the premium segment of their market.

As a corporate citizen of Renton for more than 80 years, PACCAR has traditionally supported many civic endeavors, including the arts. In 1969 the company gave the city a substantial grant to construct the Carco Theatre. PACCAR also donated $10,000 in 1988 to the Renton Historical Museum to help establish a permanent exhibit on the city's history. Throughout the years employees have been actively involved in various civic and service organizations.

During the 1940s the Pacific Car Company converted its Renton railcar production facilities to a plant for the production of tanks. By the end of World War II more than 900 Sherman tanks had been built at the Renton site.

HIGHLANDS COMMUNITY CHURCH

"The foundation of the congregation is based upon Scripture, and the focus of the people is on the Lord. We believe that every community should have such a foundation with such a focus," states pastor Wallace R. Wilson. His statement has proved to be the cornerstone for the church that he and his wife, Inez, began in 1946 at the request of a small group of would-be parishioners. From that congregation of six led by Pastor Wilson, the Highlands Community Church at 3031 Northeast 10th Street in Renton was formed. Its membership swelled so that now approximately 1,000 attend on any given Sunday and contact with 3,000 others is maintained via the church's mailing list.

The Highlands Community Church did not exist until after World War II largely because the Highlands section of Renton was not developed until it was needed as a temporary housing project for about 10,000 people—Boeing workers and their families—who came to the area to build planes for the war effort. In the newly formed Highlands community there was a grade school, a community center, and a grocery store, but there was no church. The government gave interested people use of the gymnasium in the Highlands Administration Building and services began. A Roman Catholic mass was said early Sunday mornings, and following that the area Protestant churches took turns providing services for some 25 different denominations.

During the war years Pastor Wilson, then a student, spent his summers in Renton working with children. In 1946, a new Bible college graduate, he returned to Renton with his bride and offered a Sunday Bible school. About 300 children gathered, and it was at this time that he was approached about beginning a church for the Highlands, and he agreed.

Wallace R. Wilson, pictured here with his wife, Inez, has been the only senior pastor of the Highlands Community Church since he founded it in 1946. Pastor Wilson gives some of the credit to his wife for his longevity in the position. "No man can remain the pastor of a church for as long as I have without the support of his wife," he says.

From its inception, the Highlands Community Church was a multidenominational gathering place. Pastor Wilson stated that the community church worked because "we recognized that we all agreed on 97 percent of doctrines, and we would emphasize the areas of agreement and be understanding about the differences." This inclusive philosophy worked because, in 1957, after nine years of negotiations with the federal government to buy the land, the present site belonged to the Highland Community Church, and the building was erected the following year. Amazingly, the initial building was totally funded from within the congregation, and the actual construction was provided by the parishioners. Four years after completing the first building they were able to add an auditorium—again without loans. As the congregation grew, so did its needs. In 1974 a Family Center was constructed to house a gym and classrooms. Much of the expertise, such as the architectural plans, foreman, and brick masons, were provided by the congregation. The church currently has plans for a 1,550-seat auditorium.

The congregation of the Highlands Community Church has grown from just six members in 1946 to nearly 3,000 at present. According to senior pastor Wallace R. Wilson, attendance is "about 1,000" on any Sunday morning.

Community involvement is an important fact of life for the Highlands Community Church, and Pastor Wilson says that the church tries to be supportive of community agencies rather than be isolated from them. Often the sense of community extends far beyond the boundaries of Renton as the Highlands Community Church helps missionary efforts on every continent. This sense of unity is helped by the beliefs that they share for, according to Pastor Wilson, "The core of a community remains the same; there should be no community without the knowledge of a loving God and Christ."

SOUND CAR & TRUCK STORES

Fred Knack came to Renton late in his career. He had retired from several successful car dealerships and was "wooed" west by Ford Motor Company in February 1975. Upon arrival he purchased a prominent Rainier Avenue location now known as Sound Ford. The troubled dealership soon flourished under his careful tutelage, vast knowledge, and business acumen.

Sound Ford, located at 750 Rainier Avenue South, was Fred Knack's first Renton dealership.

Knack began his career in the automobile business as salesman in 1949 in Detroit. He purchased his first dealership in 1957 in Muskegon, Michigan. Thinking of retirement, Knack sold his dealership in 1972. After six months, deciding he did not like the inactivity of retirement, he became involved in dealerships in Corpus Christi and Houston, operating them successfully for more than two years.

It was then that Ford Motor Company approached Knack to see if he was interested in looking at the Renton dealership. Knack liked what he saw, moved to the area, and purchased what was once the Robinson-Lyon Ford dealership at Rainier Avenue and Grady Way. He later purchased two more dealerships, one in Renton (Sound Oldsmobile-GMC-Toyota), and one in Spokane (Downtown Lincoln Mercury Mazda). Since that time the total number of dealerships has grown to nine, most of them in the Renton area. Knack began his dealership with 57 employees; in the ensuing years that number has grown to 678.

Knack is a member of the Greater Renton Chamber of Commerce and has served on its board of directors for a three-year term. He is also an honorary automobile retail member of Renton Rotary.

Knack, who grew up in the Depression years and says he has been "very fortunate" in his own life, plans to share that good fortune with Renton-area students. In 1988 he presented a check for $25,000 to the Renton School District. The money will be used to provide scholarships for college-bound seniors or students headed toward vocational training at Renton Vocational Technical Institute.

"I've been very fortunate in my life," says Knack. "This city, this area, has been very good to me. I just thought I'd like to show my appreciation and return the favor."

Fred Knack enjoys his life in Renton and is proud of what he has accomplished in the area. Courtesy, Valley Daily News

Knack, born and raised in Detroit, never had a chance to go to college himself. "I was born in 1913. When I was growing up, there was no money for college. My dad didn't have it. He was working two jobs just to make ends meet. I got my education through the school of hard knocks."

Today Knack is a prominent Puget Sound area businessman whose holdings include Sound Ford, Sound Hyundai, Sound Mazda, Sound Oldsmobile-GMC-Toyota, Auburn Subaru, Sound Subaru Peugot, Sea-Tac Ford Truck Sales, Spokane Lincoln-Mercury-Mazda, and Gig Harbor Ford.

"We sold more than 21,000 units—new and used—in 1988," he says. "How many have I sold in my life? I don't have any idea. I'd be afraid to guess."

Knack credits his own success to a fair share of good people and good fortune. "We've been very fortunate in being able to hire good people. I have excellent, dedicated people," he states. "I think that has a lot to do with it—and being in the right place at the right time."

E&H PROPERTIES

Eugene Horbach's first activity in the Renton area began in 1966 when he acquired a building under construction that was completed and leased to IBM. That was the beginning of office building and leasing in a market that was then dominated by large warehousing activities. It was a new idea—trying to establish Renton as an office users' city and raising it to the stature of other suburban localities in the Seattle area.

Although considered by many as a high-risk development, the first IBM building in the Earlington Industrial Park eventually evolved into a 70,000-square-foot facility that was occupied for 13 years by IBM and then the Boeing Company. The name of the building stuck until the present day, although it has been used by different tenants since.

In the following years other projects were developed in that area occu-

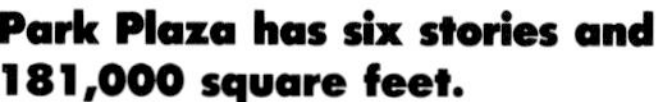

Park Plaza has six stories and 181,000 square feet.

Eugene Horbach, founder and president of E&H Properties.

A reproduction of a print commemorating the opening of the Boeing Engineering Center, an E&H Properties Development.

Garden Plaza has five stories and 250,000 square feet.

BELOW: Fifth and Park has three stories and 65,000 square feet.

pied by Collins Avionics, R.C.C, BOECON, Rockwell, Boeing, and other easily recognizable tenants.

During this time Horbach acquired lease hold interests in the Payless shopping center and other properties in the south end. In 1978 Horbach began to concentrate his activities in the area of Park Avenue North and Fourth Street adjacent to PACCAR and Boeing. In 1980 the first Class A building at 500 Park was constructed; it became known by local residents as the "Glass Palace." Subsequently, Horbach entered into a preleasing agreement with Boeing to build the area's first seven-story, state-of-the-art, building; it remains unique in its engineering features in the northwest area. The first large parking garage to maximize parking and get away from acres of ugly black asphalt was built to serve the 180,000-square-foot office building. The project was completed in November 1985.

Horbach then developed a 330,000-square-foot facility located in the Kent Valley and leased it to the Boeing Aerospace Company. The outstanding feature of this project is the 33,000-square-foot modern food service facility serving thousands of Boeing employees. To this day the two towers in

this project are the only buildings erected to high-rise specifications in the valley.

About the same time E&H Properties' attention was again directed to Renton, and the tallest building in the city was constructed at Main and Grady, becoming a landmark because of its unusual shape and choice of building materials.

In rapid progression an additional three projects were built by E&H Properties in the Duwamish and Renton areas. The Duwamish site, located in a bend of the Duwamish River, offered unusual opportunity to design one of the most beautiful office complexes in the northwest area. Its characteristic swept-wing shape has become an easily recognizable landmark on northerly approaches to the Sea-Tac Airport. In addition, two new buildings, comprising approximately 431,000 square feet and connecting garages, were erected in the Renton area near Boeing's main manufacturing facilities, providing a distinct office center for Boeing administrative and engineering staff.

Park Plaza is connected by a handsome granite-clad skybridge that joins a large garage and Park Plaza office, providing greater safety and protection from weather for Boeing employees.

Main and Grady has seven stories and 123,000 square feet.

The 600 Building has six stories and 181,000 square feet.

At the same time E&H Properties has acquired numerous properties in the Bellevue area that Horbach intends to develop as high-rise and elegant retail bases.

Over the past 25 years E&H Properties has become one of the major real estate developers in the Pacific Northwest. A major portion of its real estate holdings are leased to Boeing, and in 1989 Horbach was recognized by Boeing as its number-one developer.

Recently he has diversified into the health care industry, having acquired controlling interest in eight health care and home health care companies located throughout the United States and Europe.

As Horbach watches Renton emerging as one of the premier new centers for business and industry development, he is convinced that there is a bright future for the city, and he takes personal satisfaction that he is a part of that vision. He hopes to bring additional recognition to the City of Renton, through his efforts in aesthetically pleasing and environmentally sound designs of projects.

This makeshift fishing hole, located behind the Everett Culver homestead in the northern section of Renton known as Kennydale, provided many hours of outdoor enjoyment for both adults and children. Courtesy, Renton Historical Society and Museum

The picturesque Cedar River, depicted here in the early 1900s before it was straightened and dredged, still runs through the heart of Renton. Courtesy, Renton Historical Society and Museum

Patrons

The following individuals, companies, and organizations have made a valuable commitment to the quality of this publication. Windsor Publications and the Greater Renton Chamber of Commerce gratefully acknowledge their participation in *Renton: Where the Water Took Wing.*

A&H Stores, Inc.*
Barbee Mill*
Beadex*
The Boeing Company*
E&H Properties*
First Federal Savings and Loan Association of Renton*
Group Health Cooperative*
Highlands Community Church*
Holmes Electric Company*
Olympic Pipe Line Company*
PACCAR Inc*
Renton Coil Spring Company*
Seattle Lumber Company*
Sound Car & Truck Stores*
Tonkin Family Restaurants*
U S WEST Communications*
Valley Medical Center*
S. John Vukov, M.D.*
Washington Natural Gas*

*Partners in Progress of *Renton: Where the Water Took Wing*. The histories of these companies and organizations appear in Chapter 7, beginning on page 97.

The Alki bar on Third and Main was typical of the saloons in early Renton. A 1904 newspaper advertisement, however, noted for the discriminating drinker that the bar served "Bohemian and Tannhauser beer on draught." Courtesy, Renton Historical Society and Museum

Annotated Bibliography

The materials I used to research this book are to be found in several locations. The most comprehensive collection of historical and topical material is that found in the Renton Historical Museum's library and archives. There is also a considerable amount in the Suzzallo Library Special Collection at the University of Washington in Seattle. The Renton Public Library also has historical material in its Pacific Northwest Collection. Locations I explored only briefly but which promise great reward for those who would devote more time are the City Records Department and the Engineering Department at Renton's city hall.

For further reading I would suggest the following books. One should begin with a general history of the King County area. Although dated, the best is Clarence Booth Bagley's *History of King County* (Chicago-Seattle: The S.J. Clarke Publishing Company, 1929). Bagley's *History of Seattle* (Chicago: The S.J. Clarke Publishing Company, 1916) also touches upon the area's early history. Although even older than Bagley's, Hubert Bancroft's work, *The Works of Hubert Howe Bancroft, Volume XXXI: History of Washington, Idaho and Montana, 1845-1889* (San Francisco: The History Company, Publishers, 1890) provides much early information about pioneer politics and mining. Another good general history is Cornelius Holgate Hanford's *Seattle and its Environs,* (Chicago and Seattle: Pioneer Historical Publishing Co., 1924). More recently, histories of coal towns near Renton have been written, such as Richard K. and Lucile McDonald's *The Coals of Newcastle: A Hundred Years of Hidden History* (Washington: Issaquah Alps Trails Club, 1987) and Diane and Cory Olson's *Black Diamond: Mining the Memories* (Seattle: Frontier, 1988). A useful chronicle of the Cedar River valley is Morda Slauson's *One Hundred Years On The Cedar* (Seattle: The Shorey Book Store, 1971). A recent history of Lake Washington and its encircling towns is Lucile McDonald's *The Lake Washington Story* (Seattle: Superior Publishing Co., 1979). A history of Bellevue, also by McDonald, is *Bellevue: Its First 100 Years* (Fairfield, Washington: Ye Galleon Press, 1984). The early development of Renton Airport is examined in *Bryn Mawr: 1872-1986* by Harold "Jiggs" Hoyt (Shohomish: Shohomish Publishing Co., 1986).

The product of decades of collecting historical lore about Renton is Morda Slauson's *Renton: From Coal to Jets* (Renton Historical Society, 1976). A slimmer, more recent work is by Paul Rowe and Jack R. Evans, *Renton, Washington* (Seattle: SCW Publications, 1987). An interesting look at Renton near the turn of the century is *Renton: The Town of Payrolls* (Renton Chamber of Commerce, 1910). A similar piece of boosterism, but interesting for its 1950s photos, is *Renton, Washington: Home of the Famous 707* (Republic Publications, 1957). More recent is *The Renton Story,* printed for the Renton Diamond Jubilee 1901-1976.

Two popular books that touch upon the geology of the area are Bates McKee's *Cascadia: The Geologic Evolution of the Pacific Northwest* (New York: McGraw-Hill Book Company, 1972); and David Alt's and Donald W. Hyndman's *Roadside Geology of Washington* (Missoula, Montana: Mountain Press Publishing Company, 1984). Another source dealing with local geology is Marvin A. Pistang's *Bedrock and Bootsoles: An Introduction to the Geology of the Issaquah Alps* (Issaquah: Issaquah Alps Trails Club, 1981). A more detailed examination of the Renton area's coal formations is found in George Evans' *The Coal Fields of King County* (Olympia: Washington Geological Survey Bulletin No. 3, 1912). A fascinating, comprehensive year-by-year examination of the coal mines in Renton and its sister coal towns is in the Washington Coal Mine Inspector *Report* (Olympia: Frank M. Lamborn, Pub.), published annually.

There is as yet no published history of the Duwamish people, but some material about them is available. Two are archaeological reports by Dr. James C. Chatters, *Archaeology of the Sbabadid Site 45KI51, King County, Washington* (Seattle, University of Washington: Office of Public Archaeology, 1981); and *Tualdad Altu (45KI59)* (Seattle: First City Equities, 1988). Several Duwamish myths are preserved in Arthur Ballard's "Puget

Sound Mythology," *University of Washington Publications in Anthropology,* Vol. 3, (Seattle, 1929), and information about the Duwamish "spirit-canoe" ceremony can be found in Thomas Talbot Waterman's "Paraphernalia of the Duwamish 'Spirit-Canoe' Ceremony" in *Indian Notes,* No. 7 (New York: Heye Foundation, 1930). For an account of their life on the Black River, I offer my own article "The Life and Death of the Black River" in *The Weekly* (Seattle: Sasquatch Press) October 15-22, 1985. The valuable testimony mentioned in the book is in *Duwamish, Lummi, Whidbey Island, Skagit, Upper Skagit, Swinomish, et al. Tribes of Indians v. U.S.A. Court of Claims of the United States.* LXXIX, 530. Wash., D.C.: Govt. Printing Office, 1935., and reprinted in two volumes by the Argus Press, Seattle.

An interesting account of black coal miners in the area is Ernest Moore's *The Coal Miner Who Came West* (Northwest Advertising, Inc., 1982). A comprehensive history of Renton's schools is Oliver M. Hazen's *A History: Renton School District 403* (Renton, 1976). The rise of Pacific Car and Foundry is examined in Alex Groner's *PACCAR: The Pursuit of Quality* (Bellevue, Washington: Documentary Book Publishers, Co., 1981), and two of the many books about the Boeing Company are Michael J.H. Taylor's *Plane Makers: Boeing* (London: Janes Publishing Company, 1982), and Harold Mansfield's *Vision: The Story of Boeing: A Saga of the Sky and the New Horizons of Space* (New York: Duell, Sloan & Pearce, 1966). An account of the area's largest private utility, edited by Robert E. Wing, is *Century of Service: The Puget Power Story* (Bellevue, Washington: Puget Sound Power and Light, 1987).

The interior of Tom Harvies' grocery store reflects the needs of early settlers—a little bit of everything, but lots of basics like brooms and blankets. Courtesy, Renton Historical Society and Museum

Index

This book was set in Times and Futura type and printed on 70 lb. Mead enamel.

Printing and binding by Walsworth Publishing Company.